INTRODUCING
ISSUES WITH
OPPOSING
VIEWPOINTS®

The Election Process

Mike Wilson, *Book Editor*

GREENHAVEN PRESS
A part of Gale, Cengage Learning

GALE
CENGAGE Learning™

Detroit • New York • San Francisco • New Haven, Conn • Waterville, Maine • London

Christine Nasso, *Publisher*
Elizabeth Des Chenes, *Managing Editor*

© 2008 Greenhaven Press, a part of Gale, Cengage Learning

For more information, contact:
Greenhaven Press
27500 Drake Rd.
Farmington Hills, MI 48331-3535
Or you can visit our Internet site at gale.cengage.com

For product information and technology assistance, contact us at

Gale Customer Support, 1-800-877-4253
For permission to use material from this text or product, submit all requests online at www.cengage.com/permissions

Further permissions questions can be emailed to permissionrequest@cengage.com

Articles in Greenhaven Press anthologies are often edited for length to meet page requirements. In addition, original titles of these works are changed to clearly present the main thesis and to explicitly indicate the author's opinion. Every effort is made to ensure that Greenhaven Press accurately reflects the original intent of the authors. Every effort has been made to trace the owners of copyrighted material.

Cover image AP Images

LIBRARY OF CONGRESS CATALOGING-IN-PUBLICATION DATA

The election process / Mike Wilson, book editor.
   p. cm. — (Introducing issues with opposing viewpoints)
  Includes bibliographical references and index.
  ISBN-13: 978-0-7377-3975-6 (hardcover) 1. Elections—United States. I. Wilson, Mike, 1954–
  JK1978.I58 2008
  324.60973—dc22

                2008006557

Printed in the United States of America
1 2 3 4 5 6 7 12 11 10 09 08

Contents

Foreword

I
ndulging in a wide spectrum of ideas, beliefs, and perspectives is
a critical cornerstone of democracy. After all, it is often debates
over differences of opinion, such as whether to legalize abortion,
how to treat prisoners, or when to enact the death penalty, that shape
our society and drive it forward. Such diversity of thought is frequently regarded as the hallmark of a healthy and civilized culture. As the
Reverend Clifford Schutjer of the First Congregational Church in
Mansfield, Ohio, declared in a 2001 sermon, "Surrounding oneself
with only like-minded people, restricting what we listen to or read only
to what we find agreeable is irresponsible. Refusing to entertain doubts
once we make up our minds is a subtle but deadly form of arrogance."
With this advice in mind, Introducing Issues with Opposing Viewpoints
books aim to open readers' minds to the critically divergent views that
comprise our world's most important debates.

Introducing Issues with Opposing Viewpoints simplifies for students
the enormous and often overwhelming mass of material now available
via print and electronic media. Collected in every volume is an array of
opinions that captures the essence of a particular controversy or topic.
Introducing Issues with Opposing Viewpoints books embody the spir-
it of nineteenth-century journalist Charles A. Dana's axiom: "Fight for
your opinions, but do not believe that they contain the whole truth, or
the only truth." Absorbing such contrasting opinions teaches students
to analyze the strength of an argument and compare it to its opposition. From this process readers can inform and strengthen their own
opinions, or be exposed to new information that will change their minds.
Introducing Issues with Opposing Viewpoints is a mosaic of different
voices. The authors are statesmen, pundits, academics, journalists, corporations, and ordinary people who have felt compelled to share their
experiences and ideas in a public forum. Their words have been collected from newspapers, journals, books, speeches, interviews, and the
Internet, the fastest growing body of opinionated material in the world.

Introducing Issues with Opposing Viewpoints shares many of the well-
known features of its critically acclaimed parent series, Opposing
Viewpoints. The articles are presented in a pro/con format, allowing readers to absorb divergent perspectives side by side. Active reading questions
preface each viewpoint, requiring the student to approach the material

thoughtfully and carefully. Useful charts, graphs, and cartoons supplement each article. A thorough introduction provides readers with crucial background on an issue. An annotated bibliography points the reader toward articles, books, and Web sites that contain additional information on the topic. An appendix of organizations to contact contains a wide variety of charities, nonprofit organizations, political groups, and private enterprises that each hold a position on the issue at hand. Finally, a comprehensive index allows readers to locate content quickly and efficiently.

Introducing Issues with Opposing Viewpoints is also significantly different from Opposing Viewpoints. As the series title implies, its presentation will help introduce students to the concept of opposing viewpoints, and learn to use this material to aid in critical writing and debate. The series' four-color, accessible format makes the books attractive and inviting to readers of all levels. In addition, each viewpoint has been carefully edited to maximize a reader's understanding of the content. Short but thorough viewpoints capture the essence of an argument. A substantial, thought-provoking essay question placed at the end of each viewpoint asks the student to further investigate the issues raised in the viewpoint, compare and contrast two authors' arguments, or consider how one might go about forming an opinion on the topic at hand. Each viewpoint contains sidebars that include at-a-glance information and handy statistics. A Facts About section located in the back of the book further supplies students with relevant facts and figures.

Following in the tradition of the Opposing Viewpoints series, Greenhaven Press continues to provide readers with invaluable exposure to the controversial issues that shape our world. As John Stuart Mill once wrote: "The only way in which a human being can make some approach to knowing the whole of a subject is by hearing what can be said about it by persons of every variety of opinion and studying all modes in which it can be looked at by every character of mind. No wise man ever acquired his wisdom in any mode but this." It is to this principle that Introducing Issues with Opposing Viewpoints books are dedicated.

Introduction

"The final expression of the opinion of the people with us is through free and honest elections, with valid choices on basic issues and candidates. The secret ballot is an essential to free elections but you must have a choice before you. I have heard my husband [President Franklin Delano Roosevelt] say many times that a people need never lose their freedom if they kept their right to a secret ballot and if they used that secret ballot to the full. Basic decisions of our society are made through the expressed will of the people."

—Eleanor Roosevelt, speech delivered in Paris, France, September 28, 1948

Americans take for granted that, as Abraham Lincoln stated, our political system is a "government of the people, by the people, and for the people." However, the idea that people should have the right to govern collectively through elected representatives is something that evolved over a long period of time.

Establishing Representative Government

Democracy and representative government are not the same thing. The word "democracy" comes from Greek words *demos* (people) and *kratos* (power). Ancient Greece (6th century B.C.) had a form of direct democracy in which citizens (other than women and slaves) gathered to debate and vote upon issues directly but did not elect representatives to govern. The Roman Empire had a republic, but as a practical matter most Roman citizens lived too far from Rome to participate in the government, so it was not really representative government.

In 1265 Simon de Montfort, the sixth Earl of Leicester, convened the first elected Parliament, but without approval of the king of England. King Edward I convened the first Royal Parliament in 1275. By the end of thirteenth century, England's Parliament had two houses, one including nobility and high clergy and the other including knights and burgesses. Representative democracy took another step forward when the armies of Parliament (called "roundheads") fought the armies of the king, resulting in adoption in 1689 of the "Bill of Rights," which stated laws could only be made or repealed by Parliament.

The history and development of representative government in England, along with theories of Enlightenment philosophers such as John Locke, who held that government was legitimate only with the consent of the governed, influenced the founders of the United States. Thomas Jefferson stated in the Declaration of Independence that "governments are instituted among Men, deriving their just powers from the consent of the governed."

A primary complaint among the colonists, which contributed to the American Revolution, was that Parliament adopted laws taxing the colonies but did not allow colonists to vote for their representatives adopting such laws. The phrase "taxation without representation" became a rallying cry for the American Revolution.

Should Everyone Get to Vote?

The American Revolution resulted in a representative democracy, but not for all Americans. Neither slaves nor women could vote. Voting also often was conditioned on property ownership. This was not considered odd in light of the history of representative government. Early English Parliaments had limited voting rights to those who owned a freehold of land that brought in at least forty shillings. Benjamin Franklin famously made fun of property-ownership requirements for voting:

> Today a man owns a jackass worth fifty dollars and he is entitled to vote; but before the next election the jackass dies. The man in the meantime has become more experienced, his knowledge of the principles of government, and his acquaintance with mankind, are more extensive, and he is therefore better qualified to make a proper selection of rulers—but the jackass is dead and the man cannot vote. Now gentlemen, pray inform me, in whom is the right of suffrage? In the man or in the jackass?

Franklin was in the minority on this point, however. John Adams, reflecting a view common at the time the United States was founded, warned that eliminating property requirements for voting would only encourage other groups—such as women— to demand the vote, a result that he said would "tend . . . to confound and destroy all distinctions, and prostrate all ranks to one common level."

However, the idea of universal suffrage prevailed over time, as property requirements for voting eventually were eliminated, slaves were freed and given the right to vote (Fifteenth Amendment), and the right to vote was extended to women (Nineteenth Amendment) and those at least eighteen years of age (Twenty-sixth Amendment). Other impediments to voting over time have been removed through measures such as the Twenty-fourth Amendment, prohibiting imposition of a "poll" tax on voters, and the Voting Rights Act of 1965. Universal suffrage is now considered the norm.

Are the People Fit to Govern?

Eighteenth-century British statesman Edmund Burke said that "to govern according to the sense and agreement of the interests of the people is a great and glorious object of governance. This object cannot be obtained but through the medium of popular election, and popular election is a mighty evil."

Why would anyone think popular elections could be evil? One reason might be that the average voter may lack the knowledge, integrity, or inclination to vote wisely. Nineteenth-century philosopher John Stuart Mill pointed out in his treatise *Representative Government* that

> representative institutions are of little value, and may be a mere instrument of tyranny or intrigue, when the generality of electors are not sufficiently interested in their own government to give their vote, or, if they vote at all, do not bestow their suffrages on public grounds, but sell them for money, or vote at the beck of some one who has control over them, or whom for private reasons they desire to propitiate. Popular election thus practised, instead of a security against misgovernment, is but an additional wheel in its machinery.

However, can anyone other than average voters be trusted to make better decisions? Theodore Roosevelt both asked and answered this question in a speech in 1912 when he said:

> Are the American people fit to govern themselves, to rule themselves, to control themselves? I believe they are. . . . I believe in the right of the people to rule. I believe the majority of the plain

people of the United States will, day in and day out, make fewer mistakes in governing themselves than any smaller class or body of men, no matter what their training, will make in trying to govern them.

Though Winston Churchill once said that "the best argument against democracy is a five-minute conversation with the average voter," he also said that "democracy is the worst system of government, except all the others that have been tried." Voting is a civilized alternative to rule by violence. "Ballots," said Abraham Lincoln, "are the rightful, and peaceful, successors of bullets; . . . when ballots have fairly, and constitutionally, decided, there can be no successful appeal, back to bullets; . . . there can be no successful appeal except to ballots themselves, at succeeding elections."

Most nations today consider the right to self-governance via elections a hallmark of freedom. The Universal Declaration of Human Rights provides that the "will of the people shall be the basis of the authority of government" as "expressed in periodic and genuine elections." As you read these opposing viewpoints, consider whether elections today truly satisfy the ideal of collective governance by all of the people.

Chapter 1

Is the Election Process Meaningful?

Elementary school students say the Pledge of Allegiance while taking part in the "Promote the Vote" program that encourages students to be involved in the election process.

Elections Are the Foundation of Democracy

U.S. Department of State

"Democratic elections . . . determine the leadership of the government."

The U.S. Department of State argues in the following viewpoint that democratic elections are the foundation of democracy. The author defines democratic elections to be those that are competitive, occur periodically, and include a large proportion of the adult population. The author points out that citizens also may participate in democracy directly through referendums on particular issues. Democracy, states the author, provides for peaceful transfer of power, as losers who disagree with the policies of the winners nonetheless continue to recognize the state as legitimate because of the democratic process of elections.

AS YOU READ, CONSIDER THE FOLLOWING QUESTIONS:

1. According to the author, the authority of government in a democracy is derived from what?
2. When the Constitution was signed in 1787, only which citizens had the right to vote?
3. What part of the democratic election process necessarily must be secret?

U.S. Department of State, "Elections," 2007. http://usinfo.state.gov.

Elections are the central institution of democratic representative governments. Why? Because, in a democracy, the authority of the government derives solely from the consent of the governed. The principal mechanism for translating that consent into governmental authority is the holding of free and fair elections.

All modern democracies hold elections, but not all elections are democratic. Right-wing dictatorships, Marxist regimes, and single-party governments also stage elections to give their rule the aura [atmosphere] of legitimacy. In such elections, there may be only one candidate or a list of candidates, with no alternative choices. Such elections may offer several candidates for each office, but ensure through intimidation or rigging that only the government-approved candidate is chosen. Other elections may offer genuine choices—but only within the incumbent party [the group already in power]. These are not democratic elections.

What Are Democratic Elections?

Jeane Kirkpatrick, scholar and former U.S. ambassador to the United Nations, has offered this definition: "Democratic elections are not merely symbolic. . . . They are competitive, periodic, inclusive, definitive elections in which the chief decision-makers in a government are selected by citizens who enjoy broad freedom to criticize government, to publish their criticism and to present alternatives."

What do Kirkpatrick's criteria mean? Democratic elections are *competitive*. Opposition parties and candidates must enjoy the freedom of speech, assembly, and movement necessary to voice their criticisms of the government openly and to bring alternative policies and candidates to the voters. Simply permitting the opposition access to the ballot is not enough. Elections in which the opposition is barred from the airwaves, has its rallies harassed or its newspapers censored, are not democratic. The party in power may enjoy the advantages of incumbency, but the rules and conduct of the election contest must be fair.

Democratic elections are *periodic*. Democracies do not elect dictators or presidents-for-life. Elected officials are accountable to the people, and they must return to the voters at prescribed intervals to seek their mandate to continue in office. This means that officials in a democracy must accept the risk of being voted out of office. The one exception is judges who, to insulate them against popular pressure and help ensure their impartiality, may be appointed for life and removed only for serious improprieties.

Elections Must Be Inclusive

Democratic elections are *inclusive*. The definition of citizen and voter must be large enough to include a large proportion of the adult population. A government chosen by a small, exclusive group is not a democracy—no matter how democratic its internal workings may appear. One of the great dramas of democracy throughout history has been the struggle of excluded groups—whether racial, ethnic, or religious minorities, or women—to win full citizenship, and with it the right to vote and hold office. In the United States, for example, only white male property holders enjoyed the right to elect and be elected when the Constitution was signed in 1787. The property qualification disappeared by the early 19th century, and women won the right to vote in 1920. Black Americans, however, did not enjoy full voting rights in the southern United States until the civil rights movement of the 1960s. And finally, in 1971, younger citizens were given the right to vote when the United States lowered the voting age from 21 to 18.

FAST FACT

Of persons aged eighteen to twenty-four, 46.7 percent voted in the 2004 elections.

Democratic elections are *definitive*. They determine the leadership of the government. Subject to the laws and constitution of the country, popularly elected representatives hold the reins of power. They are not simply figureheads or symbolic leaders.

Citizen Referendums

Finally, democratic elections are not limited to selecting candidates. Voters can also be asked to decide policy issues directly through referendums and initiatives that are placed on the ballot. In the United States, for example, state legislatures can decide to "refer," or place, an issue directly before the voters. In the case of an initiative, citi-

Elections including candidates from different parties and even those running as independents are vital to maintaining a democratic government.

zens themselves can gather a prescribed number of signatures (usually a percentage of the number of registered voters in that state) and require that an issue be placed on the next ballot—even over the objections of the state legislature or governor. In a state such as California, voters confront dozens of legislative initiatives each time they vote—on issues ranging from environmental pollution to automobile insurance costs.

Population and Eligible Voters by Race and Ethnicity

Race/Ethnic Group	Total Population	Percentage That Are Eligible to Register to Vote
All Races	294,856,000	68 percent
White	196,805,000	77 percent
Black	37,117,000	65 percent
Asian	14,713,000	51 percent
Hispanic	43,999,000	39 percent

People are ineligible to vote if they are not yet of voting age or if they are adults and not citizens.

Taken from: Pew Hispanic Center, 2006.

Democratic Ethics and the Loyal Opposition

Democracies thrive on openness and accountability, with one very important exception: the act of voting itself. To cast a free ballot and minimize the opportunity for intimidation, voters in a democracy must be permitted to cast their ballots in secret. At the same time, the protection of the ballot box and tallying of vote totals must be conducted as openly as possible, so that citizens are confident that the results are accurate and that the government does, indeed, rest upon their "consent."

One of the most difficult concepts for some to accept, especially in nations where the transition of power has historically taken place at the point of a gun, is that of the "loyal opposition." This idea is a vital one, however. It means, in essence, that all sides in a democracy share a common commitment to its basic values. Political competitors don't necessarily have to like each other, but they must tolerate one another and acknowledge that each has a legitimate and important role to play. Moreover, the ground rules of the society must encourage tolerance and civility in public debate.

Peaceful Transfer of Power

When the election is over, the losers accept the judgment of the voters. If the incumbent party loses, it turns over power peacefully. No matter who wins, both sides agree to cooperate in solving the common problems of the society. The losers, now in the political opposition, know that they will not lose their lives or go to jail. On the contrary, the opposition, whether it consists of one party or many, can continue to participate in public life with the knowledge that its role is essential in any democracy worthy of the name. They are loyal not to the specific policies of the government, but to the fundamental legitimacy of the state and to the democratic process itself.

As the next election comes around, opposition parties will again have the opportunity to compete for power. In addition, a pluralistic society, one in which the reach of government is limited, tends to offer election losers alternatives for public service outside government. Those defeated at the polls may choose to continue as a formal opposition party, but they may also decide to participate in the wider political process and debate through writing, teaching, or joining one of many private organizations concerned with public policy issues. Democratic elections, after all, are not a fight for survival but a competition to serve.

EVALUATING THE AUTHOR'S ARGUMENTS:

The viewpoint you just read states that elections must extend the right to vote to a large proportion of the adult population in order to be, in the author's view, "democratic" elections. If only a small percentage of voters vote, do you think that makes the elections not "democratic"? Why or why not?

Elections Are Meaningless

Patrick McKnight

Patrick McKnight argues in the following viewpoint that voting is irrelevant. No matter who wins, he says, nothing changes. He argues that two corrupt parties control government and voters are reduced to choosing the lesser of two evils. Instead the author encourages voters to cast ballots for someone they identify with—doing so will not change anything, but at least it sends a message. McKnight is a Rutgers College student who writes for the *Daily Targum*.

> *"Vote. Or don't vote. It doesn't really matter."*

AS YOU READ, CONSIDER THE FOLLOWING QUESTIONS:
1. Rather than writing to congressmen, who does the author say people should try to influence if they want change?
2. According to the author, why do politicians not pay attention to the issues that matter to young people?
3. The author claims that on February 15, 2003, the largest worldwide protests in history had no effect on what significant event?

There is a bumper sticker that says "Don't vote, it only encourages them." I know a lot of people who don't vote because they've become totally disillusioned by the rhetoric, partisanship and relentless demonizing that passes for politics these days. I wish I could say I blame them. It's a sad commentary on American democracy that elections have been reduced to picking "the lesser of two evils." Wouldn't it be nice to vote for candidates you could actually believe in?

No Choice and No Change

Some people love to preach about all the freedom of choice we enjoy in this country. These people need to seriously raise their standards. One day every couple years we get to make a single choice between two walking hair-dos in expensive suits. There are only two political parties that control virtually every aspect of government. Both parties consist mostly of old, rich, white men who used to be lawyers. And isn't that demographic always the life of any party? So maybe we don't really have a two party system after all. Maybe we have a one party system we over-idealistically choose to describe in two-party terms.

But it's the principle of the thing, I plead with them. Make your voice heard and all that nonsense. Look at how close hugely important recent elections have been. But again, it doesn't even matter all that much who wins. Neither party is likely to ever make any significant changes to anything substantively important. Both parties are in the hip-pocket of special interest groups

FAST FACT

About 30 percent of U.S. voters tell pollsters they don't belong to a political party.

and other campaign contributors. If you want to talk to the people with real influence don't waste your time writing your congressmen. Save your stamps for the power elite that get them elected in the first place.

Vote Anyway to Send a Message

Still, I am going to vote and I encourage everyone to as well. Our issues don't matter to politicians because young people don't vote nearly as much as groups like the elderly do. Maybe that's why America has been

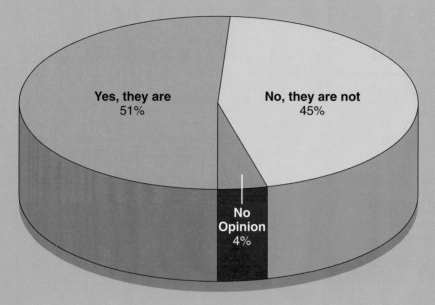

Is There a Meaningful Choice?

Whether or not you agree with them, do you think the Democrats are or are not offering the country a clear direction that is different from the Republicans?

Yes, they are
51%

No, they are not
45%

No
Opinion
4%

Taken from: *Washington Post*, October 9, 2006.

doing 50 mph in the fast lane with its turn signal on for the past 10 years. By voting you send a message to politicians telling them to at least pay our problems lip service before they do nothing to resolve them.

Another good thing about voting is you can send a message with your vote. Instead of voting against the worst candidate why not vote for someone that you actually identify with? If that's throwing my vote away so be it. At least I'm not setting it on fire and dumping its ashes in a shallow, unmarked grave which is exactly what I feel like I'm doing whenever I vote Republican or Democrat.

The System Is Corrupt

After all, everyone knows politicians regardless of party are basically nothing more than self-interested, overgrown fraternity boys with different, not larger, vocabularies. Both parties are corrupt. Both parties have the audacity to lie to our faces on a regular basis. Both parties are boring and serve no practical purpose other than to reproduce their own hypocrisies and ineptitudes. My favorite is when politicians talk about family values. Please, please stop insulting our intelligence. Even most college students have more family values in their little finger than most politicians have in their whole poll-researched list of talking points. (No congressional pages were harmed in the writing of this column).

Alternatives to Politics
Trying to change things through the American political process is like repeatedly beating your head against a huge brick wall, perhaps the Great Wall of China. Instead many young people are choosing to channel their energy and commitment to change by volunteering, advocacy and being socially conscious consumers. In *USA Today*... there was an article devoted to just this trend. It reports that in many ways Generation Y is the most civically minded group of Americans since the Baby Boomers. It notes Sept. 11 and Hurricane Katrina have

Senate Democrats appeal to lawmakers, especially Republicans, to improve the relationship between lawmakers and lobbyists after the scandal involving Jack Abramoff.

profoundly affected the way they see the world and relate to other human beings. It goes on to lament the disenfranchisement of American youth en masse from the traditional political system. But who can really blame them?

In reality many people do care. They just express this same concern in different, even opposing ways. Many people who don't vote care passionately about doing the right thing. Likewise it's not so much that Generation Y is turned off by their parents' politics as they are turned on by the new forms of activism emerging through, for example, grassroots internet efforts. Researchers need to change how they measure civic involvement to be more inclusive to these new methods of participation. Not only do older methods of activism not make any sense to younger minds neither do they continue to appear effective. On Feb. 15, 2003 the largest worldwide protests in history had no effect at all on the Invasion of Iraq. Times change.

Voting Is Just Symbolic

Not that I'm encouraging anybody to drop out of their save-the-world drum circles. Beat those peace drums until you bleed patchouli [a scent popular in the 1960s and 1970s and associated with hippies]. Nor am I telling anyone not to vote. I'm just saying that these are both mostly symbolic (translation: ineffective) ways of making a real difference. If you really want to change things then start by changing yourself. If everyone had more of their priorities in order then this whole democracy thing would take care of itself. So vote. Or don't vote. It doesn't really matter. What does matter is that as far as representation goes we all deserve much, much better.

EVALUATING THE AUTHOR'S ARGUMENTS:

After reading this viewpoint do you agree that elections provide us with no meaningful choices? Give reasons and examples for your answer.

Viewpoint

3

Negative Campaigning Informs Voters

"Negative ads tend to be more substantive than positive spots, because to be credible they must be better documented."

David Mark

David Mark argues in the following viewpoint that academics and journalists who say negative campaigning alienates voters and is antidemocratic are wrong. The author claims that most "attack ads" serve democracy by providing voters with relevant information on issues that matter. Citing historic voter turnout from past elections that involved negative campaigning, the author argues that negative attacks increase voter interest and participation. Mark is the author of *Going Dirty: The Art of Negative Campaigning.*

AS YOU READ, CONSIDER THE FOLLOWING QUESTIONS:

1. What, says the author, makes it easy for negative attacks to be immediately rebutted?
2. According to research quoted by the author, what fraction of claims in negative ads from 1960 through 2004 involved issues, not attacks on candidates' character or values?
3. According to an author quoted by Mark, enthusiasm in politics usually contains a large element of what emotion?

oliticians routinely try to shift attention away from issues of public concern, playing the victim of unfair, invasive attacks. But is closely examining a candidate's questionable financial history wrong? Senators, after all, spend hundreds of billions of taxpayer dollars. . . .

As wounded politicians whine that such speech is out of bounds, it's time to stand up in defense of the much-maligned attack ad. In this age of instantaneous information via blogs, round-the-clock cable coverage, and other media, political attacks can be swiftly countered. Any opinion offered about a candidate, no matter how mean, vile, or sinister, can be rebutted immediately and globally. Thanks to such exchanges, voters . . . will know a lot about prospective elected officials if they are willing to process multiple sources of information and draw their own conclusions. . . .

Conventional Wisdom Condemns Negative Ads

Many people recoil at negative political ads. Indeed, negative campaigning has become a catch-all phrase that implies there is something inherently wrong with criticizing an opponent. It is one of the most bemoaned aspects of the American political system, particularly by academics and journalists who say it lowers the level of discourse and intensifies divisions among voters.

FAST FACT

During the last two months of the 2006 political campaigns 90 percent of issue-based TV commercials were negative.

The dim academic view of negative campaigning was reflected in an influential 1999 *Political Science Review* study by Arizona State University political scientists Patrick J. Kenney and Kim Fridkin, titled "Do Negative Campaigns Mobilize or Suppress Turnout? Clarifying the Relationship Between Negativity and Participation." "Our most troubling finding is that negative or attack advertising actually suppresses turnout," Kenney and Fridkin wrote. "We would even go so far as to say that negative advertisements may pose a serious antidemocratic threat."

Journalists often reach similar conclusions. Take the 2006 California Democratic gubernatorial primary [to elect the governor], during

TAKING MONEY *OUT* OF YOUR POCKET

The average employee works for 116 days just to pay for one year's taxes. That hurts families.

Unfortunately, Congressman **Leonard Boswell voted AGAINST** meaningful tax relief, which would make tax rates for working Iowans go up.

And Boswell's vote would also make the per child tax credit go down — forcing families to pay more in taxes.

(Source: Roll Call Vote 135, 5/10/06)

CONGRESSMAN LEONARD BOSWELL
TAXING ON FAMILIES —
OVER AND OVER AGAIN.

Some believe that voters can learn more about a candidate through negative campaign ads sponsored by an opponent or special interest groups.

which the tactics of candidates Phil Angelides, the state treasurer, and Steve Westly, the state controller, prompted intense criticism. Each sought the right to face off against Republican Gov. Arnold Schwarzenegger, and the campaign run-up to the June primary quickly devolved into a series of harsh verbal exchanges about the candidates' environmental records, proclivity [inclination] to raise taxes, and other issues. Angelides won the primary but earned the ire [anger] of editorialists for going negative. Among the critics was Martin F. Nolan, a former reporter and editor for *The Boston Globe*, who wrote in a *San Francisco Chronicle* op-ed piece shortly after the race, "Negative campaigning reduces turnout and alienates occasional voters who would otherwise consider voting for a fresh face."

Negative Ads Are Factual

This conventional wisdom is dead wrong, argues the Vanderbilt political scientist John Geer, author of the 2006 book *In Defense of Negativity: Attack Ads in Presidential Politics.* "Journalists and academics think of negative campaigning as personal attacks," says Geer. "I don't particularly worry about it. It's going to take something a little more consequential to hurt this country than some rough 30-second spots."

Geer's research demonstrates that negative ads tend to be more substantive than positive spots, because to be credible they must be better documented and specific. His analysis of television campaign advertising from 1960 through 2004 found that nearly three-quarters of the claims in negative spots involved issues, not attacks on candidates' characters or values. "You can't just attack President Bush for being weak on the economy," Geer says. "You need to be more specific when you attack. You have to say why. For the attacks to work, they have to be based on fact."

Negative Ads Boost Turnout

There is considerable reason to believe the electorate appreciates negative campaigning. While studies like Kenney and Fridkin's suggest the practice can turn voters off, voting participation statistics demonstrate that the toughest, most partisan races often bring more people to the polls. The 2004 presidential campaign was one of the most heated in recent memory, punctuated by thrusts and parries [referring to moves in fencing, attacks and defenses] over Sen. John Kerry's Vietnam service, charges of deadly policy failures in Iraq, and warnings that electing the opposition could lead to further terrorist attacks. That same campaign produced a voter turnout of roughly 60 percent, the highest in 36 years. Kerry's vote total was up 16 percent from Vice President Al Gore's in 2000; President George W. Bush's vote total was 23 percent higher than it had been four years before.

Estimates for Political Advertisement Spending in the 2008 Elections

U.S. Senate:

Candidate $220–$250M
Party $60–$100M
Independent Expenditures $10–$20M

U.S. House:

Candidate $200–$230M
Party $100–$160M
Groups $20–$50M

State and Local:

Governors $90–$110M
Ballots $190–$230M
Judges/AG $50–$60M
Other $175–$250M

Issue:

$330–$400M

Presidential Race:

Candidate $400–$460M
Party $150–$175
Group $100–$140M

Taken from: TNS Media Intelligence/CMAG, 2007.

Those numbers fit a historical pattern. Turnout rose during the years following the Civil War, when campaigns were very biting. This was a period when Republicans were accused of "waving the bloody shirt" from the military conflict of recent memory and Democrats were labeled "disloyal" for supporting the Confederacy, or at least being lukewarm on maintaining the Union.

Or consider the infamous 1984 grudge match of a Senate race in North Carolina, where incumbent Republican Jesse Helms faced a stiff challenge from moderate Democratic Gov. Jim Hunt. The candidates raised large sums of money to pay for a full menu of negative campaign tactics: personal attacks, below-the-radar smears by allies, a series of combative debates. For that vitriolic campaign 68 percent of registered voters turned out at the polls. A more modest 60 percent cast ballots in the state's 2004 senatorial race, which coincided with the heated presidential battle. The state's prior Senate race, an open seat contest during the 2002 midterm elections, brought out a measly 40 percent of registered Tar Heel [a nickname for North Carolina] voters.

As Michael Barone, co-author of the *Almanac of American Politics*, noted shortly after the 2004 election, "Enthusiasm in politics usually contains a large element of hatred.". . .

Ugliness or Truth?

Few if any officeholders will openly admit to negative campaigning. To candidates, criticizing an opponent's voting record is properly called comparative advertising, and spotlighting a rival's marital infidelity is merely raising character issues. Campaign tactics that to one voter seem misleading, mean-spirited, or immoral can impart to another important and relevant information about how the candidate would perform under the pressures of public office. Negative campaigning, like beauty, is in the eye of the beholder.

EVALUATING THE AUTHOR'S ARGUMENTS:

Do you agree with the author that an increase in negativity causes increased voter turnout? Instead, could increased voter interest prompt increased negativity? Give reasons for your answer.

Negative Campaigning Misinforms Voters

The Economist

"Distorting your opponent's record is easy."

In the following viewpoint the author argues that negative campaigning is used to mislead voters and distort the record of candidates. Negative campaign ads, says the author, greatly outnumber nonnegative, and both Republicans and Democrats employ them. Both parties, it is claimed, try to create scandals by recording everything opponents say and do, then publicizing mistakes. Personal attacks, says the author, have been part of American politics since the Declaration of Independence. The *Economist* is a magazine covering global, domestic, and business news.

AS YOU READ, CONSIDER THE FOLLOWING QUESTIONS:
1. What percentage of ads are negative, according to the author, as polling day nears?
2. What did the Federalists accuse Thomas Jefferson of being that might be considered a personal attack?
3. Why is it easy to distort an opponent's views using voting records?

"The facts are that since Bob Humpty went to Washington, more than 350 million people around the world have died from various causes, including disease, famine, earthquakes and machete attacks. Coincidence? Not according to these realistic-looking headlines." That attack ad was dreamed up by Dave Barry, a comedian. But are the real ones much better?

Their logic is often equally strained. For example: "During Deborah Pryce's congressional tenure, gas prices have more than doubled," one learns from a website called www.badpryce.org. Deborah Pryce is the Republican representative for Ohio's 15th district. Oil traders rarely cite her influence when trying to explain why prices go up or down, but you never know.

Twisting the Record

With only a month to go before the [2006] mid-term elections, the slurs are splatting like tomatoes at a Spanish tomato-throwing fiesta. An early contender for the lowest-blow award is Vernon Robinson, the Republican challenger for a House seat in North Carolina, who produced a video alleging that his opponent, Brad Miller, "pays for

sex, but not for body armour for our troops." Mr Miller "voted to spend your money to study the sex lives of Vietnamese prostitutes in San Francisco," not to mention "the masturbation habits of old men" and "something called the Bisexual, Transgendered and Two-Spirited Aleutian Eskimos, whoever they are."

Well, sort of. Mr Miller did miss a vote on appropriations for the war in Iraq, but only because he was on his way to Iraq to visit the troops. As for the kinky stuff, Mr Robinson is referring to Mr Miller's vote not to micromanage the National Institutes of Health's budget for research into sexually-transmitted diseases. So perhaps he is not a callous pervert. But you should not vote for him anyway, because he wants to turn America into "one big fiesta for illegal aliens and homosexuals," including those who burn the American flag.

FAST FACT

Eighty percent of Americans say that negative political campaigns bother them very much or somewhat.

Negative Outnumbers Positive

In American politics, the constitutional guarantee of free speech trumps most other considerations, libel [the act of publishing false statements] included. The only real check on attack ads is that if they sound too shrill, voters may recoil. But neither party seems unduly worried about this. In the early stages of the campaign, many candidates ran positive ads to introduce themselves. But as polling day nears, most ads—90%, by some guesses—have turned negative.

Republicans charge that Democrats are soft on terrorism, crime and border security. Democrats claim that Republicans are corrupt, incompetent, beholden to big corporations and marching in lockstep with President Bush. Some ads are paid for by the candidates themselves, but many of the most bare-knuckle messages are funded by independent "527" groups such as MoveOn.org (which bashes Republicans) and the Economic Freedom Fund (which bashes Democrats).

Such groups have mushroomed since a campaign-finance reform in 2002 curbed large donations to political parties. The money simply shifted to the 527s (the term refers to the relevant article of the

Senator John McCain holds a copy of a newspaper ad sponsored by MoveOn.org criticizing General Petraeus's actions in Iraq.

tax code). For the parties, this is a mixed blessing. On the one hand, they have no control over what independent groups say on their behalf. On the other, they can plausibly distance themselves from the more underhand attacks on their opponents.

For example, MoveOn has released a series of ads in which four Republicans in marginal seats are described as "caught red-handed." To illustrate their red-handedness, MoveOn paints their hands red. It also adds a gratuitous picture of Jack Abramoff, a convicted fraudster. Yet none of the four has done anything illegal.

Slurs and Scandals

Personal attacks have long been part of American politics. The Declaration of Independence had some choice things to say about George III. Federalists called Thomas Jefferson an "atheist" and his followers "cut-throats who walk in rags and sleep amid filth and vermin." In the 1960s, a Democrat ad hinted that Barry Goldwater might start a nuclear war. Modern campaigns are probably no worse than the old ones, but several things have changed.

First, campaigns now wallow in cash—the two parties have spent $500 million between them so far on this year's [2006] race, according to Political Money Line, a watchdog. Second, the proliferation of media gives campaigners more options for getting out their message, but makes it harder to be heard above the hubbub. Both parties try to create scandals by sending flunkies to film everything their opponents say or do, and then posting gaffes [mistakes] on the internet. This works—as George Allen, the junior senator from Virginia, discovered when he used a racial slur for the man filming him. It also kills spontaneity on the campaign trail.

Lastly, both parties try to find out as much as possible about individual voters so as to target them more precisely. If, for example, someone has signed a petition calling for a bond issue to finance local schools, a candidate might tell him that his opponent will cut spending on education. Distorting your opponent's record is easy: congressmen often have to vote yes or no to omnibus [including many different things] bills with hundreds of loosely-related provisions, so they can all be portrayed as having backed a provision that, on its own, they would have shunned.

EVALUATING THE AUTHOR'S ARGUMENTS:

After reading this viewpoint, and based upon what you have seen and heard from politicians, do you agree that politicians distort the record of other candidates? Do you think such distortion sways voters? Give reasons for your answers.

Viewpoint

5

Money Decides Who Wins Elections

Andrew Greeley

"The voters don't decide any more. . . . The fat cats in both parties make the decisions."

In the following viewpoint Andrew Greeley argues that money decides who wins elections. Greeley claims rich contributors, through their contributions, rather than voters, decide who will be nominated and elected. Freedom of speech rights, he argues, prevent meaningful restriction of campaign contributions, resulting in billions of dollars spent to advertise a candidate's views and to smear and play dirty tricks on opponents. Greeley is a Catholic priest, an author, and a columnist for the *Chicago Sun-Times.*

AS YOU READ, CONSIDER THE FOLLOWING QUESTIONS:
1. Experts quoted by the author predict the 2008 presidential campaign will cost how much in campaign expenditures?
2. According to experts cited by the author, how much will the winning 2008 presidential candidate spend to get elected?
3. How, according to the author, did Abraham Lincoln campaign for the presidency?

Y ou want to live in the White House? You can buy it for $5 billion! That's what the experts say the campaign of '08 will cost. It will be split between parties and within the parties and among candidates, perhaps $200 million, $250 million for the winning candidate.

That is a lot of money. It would pay for a month of the war in Iraq. It would double the amount of money authorized but not yet paid for the renewing of New Orleans. It might pay for an aircraft carrier or two or three, which is just what the country needs these days. It might provide shelter for the homeless or for sick kids who don't have insurance. It could back up the pensions that are being taken away from workers.

Former U.S. senate candidate Brian Schweitzer holds a handful of bills representing the tobacco money he claims was taken by incumbent Senator Conrad Burns in 1999.

Money for Dirty Tricks

Where does it go? Mostly to the media and advertising industries and to the spinners and flacks who think up dirty tricks. It pays for "research" on one's opponents with which to smear them. It also finances the yearlong drama of the election entertainment to the masses for whom the campaign is rather like a horse race, for the polls (some good, some bad) that purport to tell who's winning, and for the focus groups that tell candidates what words to use or not to use and measures the impact of their gaffes [mistakes]. It pays for the consultants—soothsayers, wizards, readers of entrails, astrologers, spell casters—whose job is to hold the candidate's hand and tell him he's making the right decisions.

FAST FACT

Less than two-tenths of 1 percent of the U.S. population gave 86 percent of all itemized campaign contributions for the 2002 elections.

My advice to candidates is to sprinkle pollsters, spinners, consultants, focus group leaders and researchers with holy water and mutter appropriate prayers of exorcism.

It has been a long time since Abraham Lincoln went home to Springfield after he was nominated at the "Wigwam" in Chicago and sat on the front porch throughout the election campaign. In those days it was believed appropriate for the candidate not to campaign at all. No one suggested that endurance of the water torture of a campaign was a measure of how a man might stand up to the pressure of the White House. . . .

You find out what a person's character is by how he acts during a circus devised by homicidal maniacs?

Big Money Deciding the Winner

The commentators who offer wisdom for the masses frequently predict outcomes on the basis of how much money a given candidate may have amassed before a campaign is announced, as in asserting that Sen. Hillary Clinton has the Democratic nomination virtually in hand because of the size of her war chest. Now, I personally like the senator and think she'd make a good president (all hate mail on the subject will be deleted), but such comments demonstrate the folly of American politics. The voters don't decide any more, but the fat cats in both parties make the decisions by their contributions and pass the word on to us plebes. Ordinary folks, it is said, who own a computer can make small online contributions that collectively can outweigh the gold of the petro [oil] or pharma [drug company] barons. And the moon is made of blue cheese.

Voluntary Limits Will Not Work

There doesn't seem to be much that can be done about this immoral extravaganza of soiled gold. The Supreme Court continues to believe most restrictions on campaign contributions violate freedom of speech. The candidates could agree to voluntarily limit contributions and eschew all negative campaigning (such as suggesting that Sen. Barack Obama went to a terrorist school). They could resolutely commit

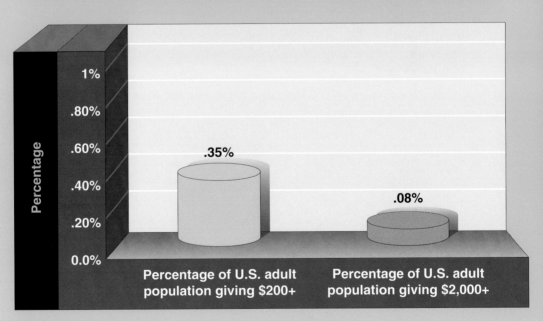

Donors of Campaign Contributions, 2005–2006

Most of the money used to finance political campaigns comes from a very small group of people.

Taken from: www.opensecrets.org/overview/DonorDemographics.asp?cycle=2006.

themselves to restrain their pollution of the atmosphere by capping the amount of aviation fuel they expend in madcap dashes around the country.

All of these steps would require self-restraint—and trust that their rival would honor the agreement. It would also mean that they would repudiate the support of unofficial groups who intervene in the campaign, allegedly on their own initiative. Most of these suggestions are pipe dreams. However, one step in the right direction would be for all serious candidates to gather around the table in the old Indian Treaty room, [in the Eisenhower Executive Office Building next to the White House] and sign a solemn compact to repudiate negative campaigning—and create a board to monitor adherence to the compact. Then they could smoke the requisite peace pipe and remember what happened to the signers of treaties in that room.

EVALUATING THE AUTHOR'S ARGUMENTS:

Do you think the author overestimates the importance of money in elections? Do you believe a candidate without a great deal of money to spend has a chance to win an election? Why or why not?

Money Does Not Decide Who Wins Elections

Oxford Analytica

"Money matters most in separating the top tier of candidates from the rest of the pack, rather than dividing contenders within that tier."

In the following viewpoint Oxford Analytica argues that while early primaries and Internet fund-raising have increased campaign contributions, money does not decide who wins presidential contests. A threshold amount of money is necessary to maintain a credible campaign, says the author, creating a disadvantage for candidates who are less established or enter late, but between top-tier candidates personal campaigning, rather than money, decides elections. Oxford Analytica is an international consulting firm providing analysis and advice to business and government.

AS YOU READ, CONSIDER THE FOLLOWING QUESTIONS:

1. According to the author, the chairman of the Federal Election Commission says that no candidate is capable of being nominated for president unless he or she can raise how much money?
2. How, in the author's view, can media perceptions of fund-raising affect a candidate?
3. George W. Bush, running for the Republican presidential nomination in 2000, won the primary in Iowa despite being outspent by whom?

Oxford Analytica, "Money Does Not Win Presidential Contests," March 20, 2007. Reproduced by permission.

S enator Hillary Clinton and former President Bill Clinton on March 18, [2007], raised over 1 million dollars at a New York fundraiser for her presidential campaign. . . .

The record for presidential fund-raising will be shattered during the 2007–08 campaign cycle. The scramble for funding has begun earlier, and should be more intense, as key primary dates have been moved forward to January and early February of [2008]. . . .

Early evidence suggests that the 2008 presidential election cycle will feature record levels of fundraising by both the Democratic and Republican candidates. Even before active campaigning began in earnest [in 2007], the chairman of the Federal Election Commission (FEC) argued publicly that the capacity to raise 100 million dollars would be the implicit test of whether or not a candidate was capable of winning a major party nomination or the election in 2008. . . .

Why So Much Money?

There are a number of factors that explain the sharp rise in contributions:

1. **Wide-open field**. The 2008 presidential election is the first in the primary era (1972 onwards) without an incumbent president or vice president on a major party ticket. Therefore, both party contests are seen as 'wide-open'—and such competitive electoral battles attract more money.

2. **New techniques**. New campaign finance techniques—notably the solicitation of support via the internet pioneered by Howard Dean in 2004—have been adapted and extended. Once considered primarily as a medium for ideological or 'fringe' candidates to raise funds, internet fund-raising has entered the US political mainstream. This phenomenon will be particularly important on the Democratic side, because research indicates that a higher proportion of the party's supporters are internet-orientated than among Republicans.

3. **Early primaries**. The advance of key early primaries and caucuses to January 2008, accompanied by the decision by California (and several other states) to bring their contests forward to February 5, has altered the fund-raising schedule:

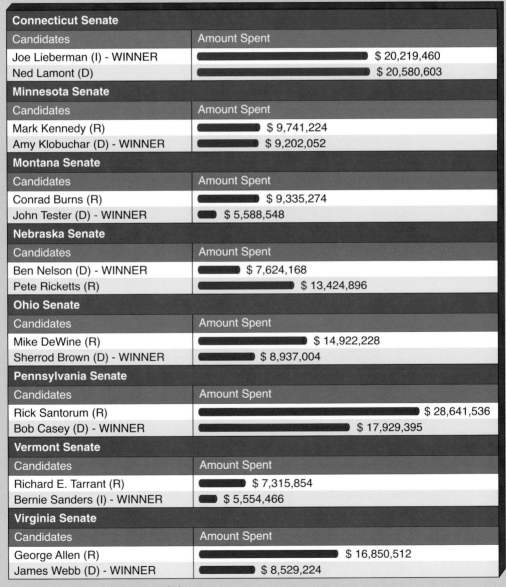

2006 Senate Races Where the Winner Spent Less than the Loser

Connecticut Senate	
Candidates	Amount Spent
Joe Lieberman (I) - WINNER	$ 20,219,460
Ned Lamont (D)	$ 20,580,603

Minnesota Senate	
Candidates	Amount Spent
Mark Kennedy (R)	$ 9,741,224
Amy Klobuchar (D) - WINNER	$ 9,202,052

Montana Senate	
Candidates	Amount Spent
Conrad Burns (R)	$ 9,335,274
John Tester (D) - WINNER	$ 5,588,548

Nebraska Senate	
Candidates	Amount Spent
Ben Nelson (D) - WINNER	$ 7,624,168
Pete Ricketts (R)	$ 13,424,896

Ohio Senate	
Candidates	Amount Spent
Mike DeWine (R)	$ 14,922,228
Sherrod Brown (D) - WINNER	$ 8,937,004

Pennsylvania Senate	
Candidates	Amount Spent
Rick Santorum (R)	$ 28,641,536
Bob Casey (D) - WINNER	$ 17,929,395

Vermont Senate	
Candidates	Amount Spent
Richard E. Tarrant (R)	$ 7,315,854
Bernie Sanders (I) - WINNER	$ 5,554,466

Virginia Senate	
Candidates	Amount Spent
George Allen (R)	$ 16,850,512
James Webb (D) - WINNER	$ 8,529,224

Taken from: www.opensecrets.org/races/index.asp.

- In the past, major contenders declared their intention to run somewhat later, spent the second, third and fourth quarters of the year before the election raising money, and only focused their campaigning on the earliest votes (in Iowa and New Hampshire) during the fourth quarter. Candidates who survived these initial hurdles sought to refill their campaign coffers between the January-February Iowa/New Hampshire contests (and the South Carolina primary for the Republicans) and the key multi-state 'super Tuesday' primaries in March.
- This traditional schedule is not practical for 2007–08 election. Serious candidates will need to raise as much money as possible throughout 2007, while actively campaigning in the early primary states—working on the assumption that they will have minimal financial 'refueling' time during the 2008 primary battle.
- However, once the major party candidates sew up the de facto nominations in February 2008, they will enjoy a longer period to campaign and secure additional funds for the general election (ahead of their formal anointment in the late summer Democratic and Republican national conventions)....

The Money Has Limited Influence

However, it is possible to draw overly broad conclusions about the impact of fund-raising on the campaign. Fund-raising considerations will have a significant, but limited, influence:

1. **Disadvantaging 'insurgents'.** The principal impact of raising the campaign 'money bar' is to increase the gap between prominent, established candidates and late-entering 'insurgent' candidates. This may make it more difficult for any [candidate] who is not [established] to launch a viable campaign. . . .

   Furthermore, given that all . . . established candidates have a strong presence on the internet, it may be difficult for new entrants to emulate Dean's 2004 on-line fund-raising surge. . . . Potential latecomers, may find that it is now impossible to launch their campaigns.

Students working on a campaign for Howard Dean use the Internet to solicit support from average Americans.

2. **Top tier parity**. Within each party's top tier relative fund-raising success may not be especially consequential—providing that critical thresholds are achieved. . . . Media perceptions of 'momentum', particularly in fund-raising, can be significant.

3. **Personal campaigning matters**. A large campaign bank account is more important after the Iowa and New Hampshire (and South Carolina) contests than in these states—where personal campaigning and organizations remain very significant. There have been numerous occasions when less financially sound candidates have won in these early tests. Senator John Kerry was probably outspent by Dean in both Iowa and New Hampshire in 2004, but he still won. Bush won in Iowa in

2000 despite probably being outspent by Steve Forbes, yet then lost in New Hampshire despite outspending McCain. This reinforces the observation that money matters most in separating the top tier of candidates from the rest of the pack, rather than dividing contenders within that tier.

The 2007 fund-raising battle will create a sharper distinction between the top tier of contenders and the rest of the pack. This may discourage 'late-entry' candidates. Money does not decide presidential races, but a lack of it can doom a campaign.

EVALUATING THE AUTHOR'S ARGUMENTS:

The viewpoint you just read highlights Internet fund-raising as a new technique for politicians trying to raise money. How do you think the Internet will impact campaign fund-raising in the future?

Chapter 2

Is the Election Process Fair and Inclusive?

Fair elections are a cornerstone of effective democracies.

Voter ID Laws Validate Voting

Meredith Togstad

"All voters should have to show photo identification before casting ballots."

In the following viewpoint Meredith Togstad contends that the integrity of the election process requires that voters present photo identification when voting. She argues that without such ID requirements, people can easily vote twice or under a pseudonym. Both parties, she says, should support photo ID requirements. The author dismisses claims that ID requirements will reduce voter turnout and claims ID requirements will make election results more reliable. Togstad writes for the *Badger Herald* in Madison, Wisconsin.

AS YOU READ, CONSIDER THE FOLLOWING QUESTIONS:

1. According to the chairman of the Republican Party of Wisconsin, as quoted by the author, how will voter ID requirements affect political culture?
2. According to polls cited by the author, voters in which party are more likely to favor ID requirements for voters?
3. According to a Rutgers professor quoted in the article, how would ID requirements affect the turnout of black voters?

As the time has come for political candidates to start rallying support for upcoming campaigns and for antsy voters to study up on their prospective policy leaders, it is no surprise that new proposals regarding fair and honest elections are in the works. The recent initiative to require Wisconsin voters to produce a valid photo ID in order to mark their ballots is necessary, appropriate and a step in the right direction toward candid and impartial elections.

Voter ID Promotes Integrity

While people can easily succeed at illegally voting twice or under a pseudonym, this obligatory plan has support from Wisconsin's senators and its Republican Party chair members. According to a press release from the Republican Party of Wisconsin on Feb. 27, [2007,] this photo ID requisite at voter registration time is needed in order to reinstate a sense of honor in Wisconsin's elections.

"The photo ID requirement is vital to the integrity of our elections in Wisconsin," Brad Courtney, chairman of the Republican Party of Wisconsin, said in the release. Mr. Courtney added that the initiative will not only restore confidence in our state's electoral process, but a feeling of unanimity among the two political parties will also result due to a reinvigorated and more honest political culture.

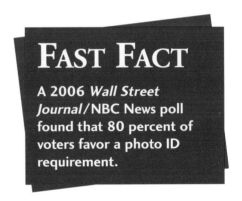

FAST FACT

A 2006 *Wall Street Journal*/NBC News poll found that 80 percent of voters favor a photo ID requirement.

"The integrity of our electoral process is an issue that should unite Republicans and Democrats, [as] it is crucial to our democratic way of life," Courtney said. I agree with Mr. Courtney and feel this hands-on approach to restoring the veracity of Wisconsin's voting process will ensure more forthright elections.

Republicans Support More than Democrats

Although the production of a legitimate photo ID requirement is backed by both political parties throughout all of the polled counties in Wisconsin, I found it interesting that the percentage of

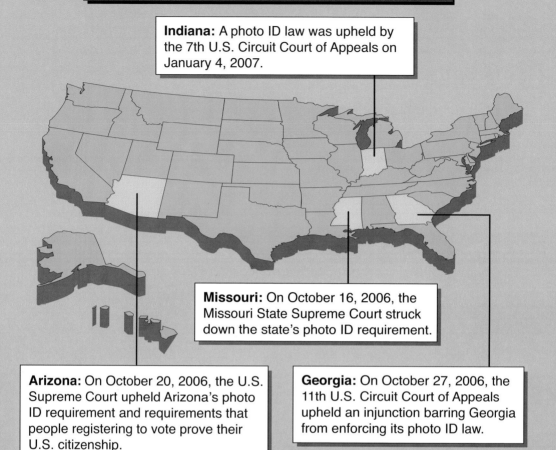

Court Decisions Concerning Voter IDs

Indiana: A photo ID law was upheld by the 7th U.S. Circuit Court of Appeals on January 4, 2007.

Missouri: On October 16, 2006, the Missouri State Supreme Court struck down the state's photo ID requirement.

Arizona: On October 20, 2006, the U.S. Supreme Court upheld Arizona's photo ID requirement and requirements that people registering to vote prove their U.S. citizenship.

Georgia: On October 27, 2006, the 11th U.S. Circuit Court of Appeals upheld an injunction barring Georgia from enforcing its photo ID law.

Taken from: National Conference of State Legislatures, February 1, 2007.

Democrats who support the requirement was much lower than that of the Republicans. According to a press release from state Sen. Mary Lazich, R-New Berlin . . . Wood Communications of Madison surveyed 500 potential voters in March 2001 on their opinions of the initiative. Fifty-five percent of likely voters who considered themselves Democrats supported the photo ID requirement while an outstanding 81 percent of those who considered themselves Republicans favored the proposal.

Despite the fact that those numbers may be different today, it is still shocking to me that there were not rave 100 percents in both columns six years ago. Yet, there is much light at the end of the tunnel, as a combined 65 percent of the 500 polled "thought all voters should have to show photo identification before casting ballots." Furthermore, Mr. Courtney feels the proposal holds much promise if more Democrats will recognize the bill's benefits: "Hopefully, the Democrats in the Senate see the light and let the photo ID requirement come up for a vote," Courtney said.

Honest and Clean Elections

With this potential cure-all initiative promising more honest and clean elections in Wisconsin, it baffles me that not all of our state's political frontrunners cannot see that the proposal's countless pros clearly outweigh its minimal cons. Apparently, it is thought that if Wisconsin voters are obliged to present a valid form of identification when they arrive at the voting booths, voter turnout rates will decrease. *Capital Times* Editor Dave Zweifel feels the photo ID requirement will cause unidentified voters to shy away from the polls. "Rutgers [University] Professor Tim Vercellotti told the *Times* that in states where voters were required to sign their names or show an identifying document, blacks were 5.7 percent less likely to vote compared to states where voters simply had to say their names,"

Georgia Governor Sonny Perdue holds up a sample of a photo voter ID after approving a bill that requires the IDs for future elections.

Zweifel reported Wednesday. He added that the push "to change existing laws" will only "make it tougher for folks to vote in an election." This passive outlook on the voting process in Wisconsin proves unacceptable; I rebuff any suggestion of a potential decline in voter turnout when the initiative at stake will only improve the status of our elections' reliability.

Consequently, I look forward to the more honest and immaculate elections Wisconsin will no doubt experience with the passage of this indispensable proposal. I say, saddle up all, both donkeys and elephants [symbols of the Democrat and Republican parties], and forbid the frauds to put the wrong candidate in any political office.

EVALUATING THE AUTHOR'S ARGUMENTS:

The author states that it is easy to vote twice or vote using a pseudonym if voter ID is not required, but does not provide any evidence or statistics to show how often this actually happens. Do you think it happens often? Why or why not? Does the author's lack of evidence influence your opinion?

Voter ID Laws Discourage Voting

Meg E. Cox

Meg E. Cox argues in the following viewpoint that voter ID laws cause more harm than good. She says the type of voter fraud such laws are supposed to prevent very rarely occurs, but that millions of voters lack a photo ID and millions of others have photo IDs but do not have a current address or current legal name. Mandatory IDs are unnecessary, she says, because identity can be proven in other ways, and few voters would risk imprisonment by signing affidavits falsifying their identity. Cox is a journalist and author.

"Requiring photo IDs would disenfranchise millions of voters."

AS YOU READ, CONSIDER THE FOLLOWING QUESTIONS:

1. How many citizens lack a government-issued photo identification, according to sources cited by the author?
2. What groups would be disproportionately penalized by photo ID requirements, according to the author?
3. How many cases of voter fraud occurred in Ohio during the 2004 elections, according to sources cited by the author?

I n Wisconsin, voter fraud is rampant. Or so thought U.S. Attorney Steven Biskupic, who began a hunt for fraudulent voters after John Kerry won Wisconsin by just 11,000 votes over George W. Bush in 2004, in an election that Republicans claimed was tainted by widespread voter fraud. But by the time he completed his work, Biskupic reported that he had uncovered no conspiracy to commit fraud. His prosecutors ended up charging only 14 people with voting illegally—and only four of them, all felons ineligible to vote, were convicted.

Texas state representative Rafael Anchia opposes a bill intended to prevent voter fraud on the grounds that it would discourage voting among minorities.

IDs Cause More Harm than Good

Lawmakers in many states are saying that there's only one way to stop this epidemic of fraud: have every voter show ID at the polls—ideally a state-issued photo ID. But experts on elections say that voter fraud of the kind that could be countered by ID requirements is rare. What's more, requiring photo IDs would disenfranchise millions of voters. The supposed remedy, these experts say, would turn out to be far worse than the actual problem.

Since 2002, the Justice Department has made an all-out effort to track down and convict fraudulent voters. By 2006, those efforts had yielded just 86 convictions nationwide, and many of those incidents, like the four Wisconsin cases, would not have been prevented by a voter ID requirement.

FAST FACT

The federal Help America Vote Act mandates that all states require identification from first-time voters who registered to vote by mail and did not provide verification of their identification with their mail-in voter registration.

Many Voters Lack ID

Meanwhile, a study by the Brennan Center for Justice found that some 21 million citizens—including a disproportionately large number of African Americans and elderly people—do not have government-issued photo ID. As many as 4.5 million people have a photo ID that lacks their current address or current legal name; many of these are young adults and people with lower income who move frequently. The proof-of-citizenship requirements that some ID advocates propose are especially onerous for married women: 32 million voting-age women do not have documents to prove citizenship that reflect their current legal name.

Proponents of strict voter ID press their case by magnifying the size of the fraud problem while minimizing the impact of voter ID laws. Ohio is one state that strengthened its ID laws after the 2004 election. The League of Women Voters teamed up with a housing advocacy group there to find out how many cases of individual voter fraud had been pursued in relation to the 2004 presidential election. They came up with a statewide total of four, or 0.00004 percent of the nearly 10 million votes cast.

Overstating Fraud

But to hear voter ID proponents tell the story, fraudulent voters were everywhere in Ohio. One master of magnification is Mark "Thor" Hearne of the American Center for Voting Rights [ACVR]. If Web presence is any indicator of an organization's legitimacy, the ACVR should raise eyebrows: its Web site didn't appear until March 2005, and it disappeared exactly two years later. But after the 2004 election, the ACVR was everywhere, testifying at hearings and filing lawsuits that claimed voter fraud.

Hearne, who was national election counsel for Bush-Cheney '04, was called to testify on behalf of the ACVR before the House Administration Committee—chaired at the time by Bob Ney (R., Ohio), who is now serving prison time for corruption—when that committee was looking into irregularities in the 2004 election. Hearne claimed that fraud was reported "in every corner" of Ohio, and that "the fraudulent voter registrations totaled in the thousands."

Hearne offered the committee this rhetorical flourish: "Ohio citizens deserve the confidence that they the voters—not trial lawyers, activist judges and special-interest groups soliciting fraudulent votes with crack cocaine—determine the result of Ohio elections." He was inspired to include the last example by the case of a hapless addict who did indeed confess to accepting cocaine in lieu [instead] of cash as payment for turning in completed registration forms. (The fraudulent forms were spotted because officials wondered why so many people with names like Mary Poppins and Michael Jackson lived on a single block and had the same handwriting. Presumably this is one of the four cases the League of Women Voters discovered. The addict was charged with a felony, and Mary Poppins didn't get to vote.)

False Analogies

Proponents of strict voter ID laws make their recommendations sound like a matter of common sense. "Every day millions of Americans show a picture ID to pay by check, board a plane or buy alcohol or tobacco," argued Vernon J. Ehlers (R., Mich.) when the U.S. House

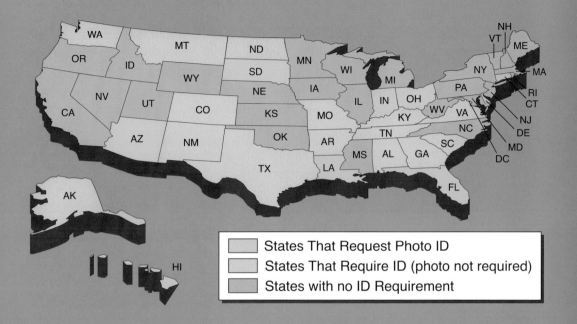

State Requirements for Voter Identification

WA, OR, MT, ND, MN, NH, VT, ME, NY, MA, ID, SD, WI, MI, PA, RI, CT, NV, WY, NE, IA, IL, IN, OH, NJ, CA, UT, CO, KS, MO, KY, WV, VA, DE, MD, AZ, NM, OK, AR, TN, NC, SC, DC, TX, MS, AL, GA, LA, FL, AK, HI

Legend:
- States That Request Photo ID
- States That Require ID (photo not required)
- States with no ID Requirement

Taken from: National Conference of State Legislatures, February 1, 2007.

was preparing its own voter ID bill. "Surely the sanctity of the ballot warrants as much protection as these other activities. Our voting rights are too important to rely on an 'honor system.'" Sound bites like these echoed from coast to coast as the bill skated through the House on a near-perfect party-line vote.

But the analogy is not accurate. First of all, it's not true that you have to have an ID to get on a plane. As George Washington University law professor Spencer Overton pointed out in an interview, "If you don't have an ID [at the airport] there's a different process, more of a search, but you don't need ID. Even in the context of terrorism there are exceptions for people flying without photo ID."

Many of the new voter ID laws, on the other hand, offer no exceptions: some states allow you to vote provisionally if you don't bring your ID to the polls, but require you to bring the ID to the board of elections within a couple of days if you want your vote counted; other states don't allow even this fallback option.

Not Just an "Honor System"

Ehlers's point about the "honor system" is also disingenuous. Most states do require voters to prove their identity in some way, and those who come to the polls without documentation can sign an affidavit [a written declaration made under oath] attesting to their identity. If suspicions of fraud surface, the affidavit becomes a tool for investigators. Penalties for voter fraud are so high that it's unlikely many individuals would be willing to risk imprisonment just to add a single vote to their favorite candidate's column.

EVALUATING THE AUTHOR'S ARGUMENTS:

The author argues that affidavits, instead of other identification, are sufficient to deter falsification of identity during elections. Do you agree? Why or why not?

"If special interest money does not acquire special interests anything at all—why would they contribute so much?"

Campaign Finance Rules Increase Political Freedom

Jay Cost

Jay Cost argues in the following viewpoint that campaign finance laws restricting "soft money" (money given to political parties rather than directly to candidates) are necessary. Interest groups donate soft money to both parties to prevent certain issues from being discussed in a public forum, undermining democracy. Such laws, he says, make it harder for moneyed interests to control legislation for their personal interest rather than for the public interest. Cost is author of a Weblog that addresses elections.

AS YOU READ, CONSIDER THE FOLLOWING QUESTIONS:

1. According to the author, moneyed interests are not buying votes but instead are buying what?
2. What law cited by the author would prevent large corporations from giving millions of dollars to political parties?
3. What is the author's view of laws restricting money dedicated to electioneering?

ormer Federal Election Commission Chair Bradley A. Smith had an interesting article in *City Journal,* which makes a libertarian-esque case against campaign finance reform. In it, he makes the following argument:

> Reformers . . . claim that reform gets rid of the political corruption that supposedly follows from large campaign contributions. Yet study after study shows that contributions play little or no role in how politicians vote. One of the most comprehensive, conducted by a group of MIT scholars in 2004, concluded that "indicators of party, ideology and district preferences account for most of the systematic variation in legislators' roll call voting behavior." The studies comport with common sense. Most politicians enter the public arena because they hold strong beliefs on public policy. Truly corrupt pols . . . want illegal bribes, not campaign donations.

As far as I know, all of the facts in this quotation are absolutely true. I have never seen any systematic evidence to indicate that contributions influence "roll call votes." However, is this the only way influence can be acquired? Absolutely not!

Moneyed Interests Control Legislation

In fact, if we look away from the congressional floor, and look instead to the committee level—we see something quite different. What we see are moneyed interests buying involvement, not votes. Moneyed

Campaign Contributions, 2005–2006 (Hard and Soft Money)

Campaign Contributions, 2005–2006 (Hard and Soft Money) in Millions of Dollars						
Donors giving:	Total	To Democrats	To Republicans	To Political Action Committees	% Democrats	% Republicans
$ 2,000+	$ 1,102.9	$ 455.6	$ 484.1	$ 218.1	41%	44%
$ 10,000+	$ 560.8	$ 251.5	$ 246.1	$ 96.7	45%	44%
$ 95,000+	$ 50.4	$ 28.3	$ 19.3	$ 5.6	56%	38%

Taken from: www.opensecrets.org, 2007.

interests spend resources to induce legislators to think positively about the issues they want them thinking positively about. In other words, moneyed interests exercise what I have . . . called the second mode of power. They help set the agenda. This is the argument of Richard Hall and Frank Wayman in their seminal article in *The American Political Science Review* called, "Buying Time: Moneyed Interests and the Mobilization of Bias in Congressional Committees." After testing their hypothesis, they conclude:

> We found solid support for our principal hypothesis: moneyed interests are able to mobilize legislators already predisposed to support the group's position. Conversely, money that a group contributes to its likely opponent has either a negligible or negative effect on their participation. While previous research on these same issues provided little evidence that PAC [political action committees] money purchased members' votes, it apparently did buy marginal time, energy, and legislative resources that committee participation requires. Moreover, we found evidence that (organized) producer interests figured more prominently than (unorganized) consumer interests in the participation decisions of House committee members—both for a case in which the issue at stake evoked high district salience [importance] and one where it did not.

We should expect something akin [similar] to this. After all, if special interest money does not acquire special interests anything at all— *why would they contribute so much?* In other words, a rational view of interests groups induces us to expect that they get something from their contributions.

Soft Money Thwarts Political Freedom

This is why the issue of campaign finance reform is not purely a First Amendment issue. Smith calls campaign finance reform a "war on political freedom." In some instances, I would agree with that. But,

Demonstrators call for a ban on soft money while Representative Christopher Shays discusses campaign finance reform.

one such area in which you will find me in staunch disagreement is the issue of soft money. If AT&T and Coca-Cola could write $50 million checks and pay for each party's political conventions—as they could before the BCRA (the Bipartisan Campaign Reform Act, a.k.a. McCain-Feingold)—it seems to me that the overall effect is one that thwarts "political freedom." If these entities are "buying time," to what extent is the government not conducting the people's business, and thus to what extent do the people actually control the actions of the government?

Soft Money Limits Public Debate

Money dedicated to the purpose of *electioneering* is money that, if restricted, limits political freedom. On this, I do not think Smith and I would disagree. However, these large soft money checks were not dedicated to electioneering. These large corporations did not give this money so that the public could hear their views, or their favored politicians' views, in the public forum. Rather, they gave large quantities of money to both parties *so as to avoid their issues being considered in the public forum.* This undermines the very nature of our democratic process.

Government Should Regulate Soft Money

And so we see the bottom line. Smith offers several anecdotal examples of the outrages of campaign finance reform. And, believe you me, I am sympathetic to all of them. Quite frankly, I think the basic premises of the Federal Elections Campaign Act (the FECA, which the BCRA replaced in 2004) are philosophically misguided and socially detrimental. It is a bad law, and—by accepting the FECA's basic view of how campaign finance should be regulated—BCRA made things worse. (Personally, I think campaign finance reform should—though it never has—promote what scholars have called responsible party government.) Nevertheless, it is just true that there are some campaign financing activities that can and do undermine our political process. In those instances, the government can and should regulate it.

I count soft money contributions to the political parties as one such instance where the government should be involved.

EVALUATING THE AUTHOR'S ARGUMENTS:

The author argues that special interest groups donate money in order to influence the legislative process. Do you think this undermines the political freedom of voters? Give reasons for your answer.

Viewpoint

4

Campaign Finance Rules Decrease Political Freedom

"[Campaign finance] reformers . . . [are] regulating only those sources of influence that they disagree with."

Bradley A. Smith

In the following viewpoint Bradley A. Smith argues that campaign finance laws hurt Republicans more than Democrats. He says there is no evidence that campaign contributions corrupt the political system. He argues that Democrats, more than Republicans, benefit from sources of influence other than campaign contributions, such as a biased press and left-leaning movie makers. Smith maintains that campaign finance reform is merely an attempt by Democrats to limit Republican political power. Smith is a former chairman of the Federal Election Commission.

AS YOU READ, CONSIDER THE FOLLOWING QUESTIONS:

1. A 1976 case, *Buckley v. Valeo,* struck down individual campaign contribution limits set forth in the 1971 campaign finance reform act on what grounds?

Bradley A. Smith, "Campaign Finance Reform's War on Political Freedom," *City Journal,* July 1, 2007. Reproduced by permission.

2. Under McCain-Feingold, incorporated organizations cannot broadcast ads that promote candidates within how many days of a federal election?
3. What movie released before the 2004 elections does the author claim was political in nature but not subject to campaign finance laws?

T his year [2007] marks the 100th anniversary of the first federal campaign finance law, the Tillman Act. Named for its sponsor, South Carolina Democratic senator Ben Tillman, the act banned corporate contributions to federal campaigns, and as such remains the backbone of federal campaign finance regulations. Tillman was a racist who advocated lynching black voters and almost single-handedly established Jim Crow in the South. The new law fit neatly with his segregationist agenda, since corporate "money power" primarily backed anti-segregationist Republican politicians.

The modern era of campaign finance reform has an equally partisan origin. From the mid-1960s on, opinion polls showed steady erosion in public support for big government and liberalism. Republicans made substantial congressional gains in 1966, and two years later Richard Nixon won the presidency. By 1970, Democrats feared—with good reason—that their longstanding electoral majority was in jeopardy. There were three ways that they might turn things around, observes Cato Institute election-law expert John Samples: persuading the public to embrace their big-government philosophy, changing that increasingly unpopular philosophy, or "preventing or at least hobbling the translation of the shifting public mood into electoral losses and policy changes."

Partisan Reason for Campaign Finance Law

The Democrats chose Number Three, and looked to campaign finance reform as a way to achieve it. The Federal Election Campaign Act (FECA), which Congress passed in 1971 (and amended three years later), would, Democrats hoped, strike at the heart of Republican political power—while leaving untouched their own sources of influence, such as union-organized volunteers. The law tightly limited both political contributions and any expenditure that might "influence" an election. It also mandated disclosure of political contributions as small as $10, established a system in which taxes financed part of presidential races, and set up a bureaucracy, the Federal Election Commission (FEC), to enforce the new rules. In *Buckley v. Valeo* (1976), the Supreme Court struck down the expenditure limits on First Amendment grounds, and held that the disclosure requirements, as well as limits on contributions to non-candidate political organizations (the National Rifle Association [NRA], say), would apply only when the group receiving the donations "explicitly advocated" the election or defeat of a candidate, through such phrases as "vote for Smith." Still, even as truncated by the Court, the new law left American politics more heavily regulated than at any time in history.

Congressional Democrats also drove the next major extension of campaign-finance regulations, the 2002 McCain-Feingold law—though of course one of the bill's cosponsors, Arizona senator John McCain, was a prominent, if unconventional, Republican. McCain-Feingold banned a kind of fund-raising in which the GOP had a growing advantage: "soft money" contributions to political parties that could fund party building and political-issue ads stopping short of

The Pennsylvania Republican State Committee filed a complaint charging that a billboard mentioning a Democratic senatorial candidate constituted an illegal corporate donation.

express advocacy. It also restricted the ability of incorporated organizations—like the NRA—to broadcast ads that so much as named a candidate within 60 days of an election, and it raised the limit on direct, "hard money" donations to candidates. Democrats were by now a Congressional minority. But enough endangered Republicans—hating the ads that targeted *them*—joined the Dems and McCain to get the bill passed.

Infringing on Freedom of Speech

The extent of the regulatory web now in place is evident even when advocates of free speech score an occasional victory. In June [2007], the Supreme Court, by a narrow 5–4 margin, held in *Federal Election Commission* v. *Wisconsin Right to Life* that the government may not prevent citizens' organizations from broadcasting ads that discuss pending legislative issues within 60 days of an election. The decision usefully prunes back one tentacle of the McCain-Feingold law. But the bulk of over 400 pages of FEC regulations remains intact. . . .

FAST FACT

The movie *Fahrenheit/911*, released four and a half months before the 2004 presidential election, grossed over $119 million dollars in the United States.

Unequal Treatment

Reformers also often claim to seek something more radical than eradicating corruption: equalizing political influence. During the debate over McCain-Feingold, numerous members of Congress repeatedly picked up on the "equality" theme. "It is time to let all our citizens have an equal voice," argued Georgia congressman John Lewis, a Democrat. Missouri senator Jean Carnahan, another Democrat, complained that "special interests have an advantage over average, hardworking citizens." Susan Collins, the liberal Republican senator from Maine, wanted "all Americans [to] have an equal voice."

Yet political influence comes in many shapes, and campaign finance reformers have little interest in equalizing all of them. Take, for example, large foundations—a major source of political influence. The assets of liberal foundations such as Carnegie, Ford, and MacArthur

Limitation on Fund-Raising Hurts Challengers

If Fundraising Declines from	And the Candidate Is	Percentage of Vote the Candidate Will Lose
$1,000 to $500 per thousand residents	Challenger	1.8%
	Incumbent	1.5%
$1,500 to $1,000 per thousand residents	Challenger	1.0%
	Incumbent	0.8%
$2,000 to $1,500 per thousand residents	Challenger	0.8%
	Incumbent	0.6%

Taken from: The Cato Institute. www.cato.org/pubs/pas/pa426.pdf.

dwarf those of their conservative counterparts: Ford's assets top $10 billion, MacArthur's $4 billion, while the Right's giant, the Bradley Foundation, commands just $500 million. Campaign finance reform leaves foundations untouched.

Laws Do Not Apply to Movies

Other important sources of influence include academia and Hollywood, both tilting to the left—and both left alone by the reformers. Consider how the law applied to Michael Moore's anti-Bush film *Fahrenheit 9/11* and to competing conservative films released in the run-up to the 2004 election. A number of complaints filed with the FEC charged Moore and others with campaign finance violations; both the movie and the advertising surrounding it, the complaints asserted, amounted to illegal contributions to the Kerry campaign. Despite Moore's public statements that he'd made his movie to help defeat Bush, the FEC dismissed all the complaints, noting, among other things, that the film was a commercial rather than a political effort.

But when the conservative organization Citizens United tried to release a film responding to many of *Fahrenheit 9/11*'s anti-Bush assertions, the FEC advised it that any public broadcast or advertising close to the election would be subject to McCain-Feingold regulations. Similarly, when Second Amendment activist David Hardy sought to release a movie before the election favoring gun rights and portraying President Bush favorably, the FEC ruled that campaign finance restrictions applied. In both cases, the FEC based its conclusion on the fact that the conservative producers, unlike Moore, weren't normally in the movie business.

Ads Can Counter Biased Media

Then there's the press—and who would deny that it has great political influence? Nevertheless, campaign finance reform leaves it unregulated thus far. More than that: as restrictions on private campaign spending grow, the free coverage that politicians get from the press becomes more and more important. And that coverage, especially coverage by the national press corps, regularly demonstrates a leftward bias, as many studies have shown. During the 2004 presidential race, the press didn't remind Americans about John Kerry's harsh criticisms of his fellow soldiers in Vietnam, or pose questions about the nature of his military service; neither did it dwell on President Bush's strong post-9/11 leadership. Those tasks, it's worth noting, were left to two conservative political organizations, Swift Boat Veterans for Truth and Progress for America, whose highly effective campaign ads engaged in the kind of political speech that campaign finance reform chokes.

Which sources of influence are regulated and which are not is a choice deeply entangled with tacit [unspoken] assumptions about who benefits from each of those sources. Despite their noble-sounding claims, reformers aren't really trying to equalize political influence: in fact, they're doing exactly the opposite, regulating only those sources of influence that they disagree with.

EVALUATING THE AUTHORS' ARGUMENTS:

Now that you have read viewpoints both pro and con regarding campaign finance laws, do you think there should be such laws? Why or why not?

Viewpoint 5

Voter Fraud Is a Real Problem

Byron York

In the following viewpoint, Byron York argues that voter fraud is real and pervasive. York cites as examples investigations in St. Louis, Washington State, and South Dakota that revealed many registered voters were actually deceased. York claims that Democrats deny voter fraud exists in order to question the legitimacy of George W. Bush's presidency. York claims Democrats are hypocritical to deny fraud, as they in recent years also have accused the Bush administration of voter fraud. York writes for *National Review* magazine.

"Voter fraud is 'widespread and insidious in the body politic.'"

AS YOU READ, CONSIDER THE FOLLOWING QUESTIONS:

1. According to Senator Christopher Bond, as quoted by the author, the number of voters registered in St. Louis threatens to exceed what number?
2. In St. Louis, what nonhuman was registered to vote?
3. In King County, Washington State, how many dead people were registered to vote, according to the author?

O n April 15, [2007,] a *New York Times* editorial declared that concerns about voter fraud—concerns that lay behind the Bush administration's firings of some U.S. attorneys—are a "fantasy." The Justice Department has investigated fraud allegations for five years, the *Times* wrote, and "has not turned up any evidence that voter fraud is actually a problem." The Bush White House was not only wrong to be worried about some prosecutors' less-than-enthusiastic pursuit of fraud allegations, the paper concluded, it was wrong to be worried at all about such a non-issue.

The Left Changes Position on Fraud

It was an extraordinary position for the *Times*, given that, two years earlier, the paper commended a group of Ohio lawyers who went to court alleging that the Bush campaign had engaged in massive voter fraud in the 2004 presidential election. The lawyers accused the Bush team of engaging in a variety of illegal acts, including a scheme in which top political strategist Karl Rove was said to have personally hacked into Ohio's electronic voting system, erasing thousands of Democratic votes. The lawyers had no evidence to support their allegations—the *Times* conceded that—but the paper said they had performed a public service by making the charges, because they had raised "concerns that many voters shared."

The *Times*'s change of heart is by no means unique on the left. A few days before the 2004 election, Markos Moulitsas, the influential Democratic blogger/activist, warned about a "nationwide" wave of voter fraud. The day after the election, another influential Democratic blogger/activist, Josh Marshall, advised John Kerry not to concede, because "this whole contest has been too dirty, too marred with voter suppression, dirty tricks and other unspeakable antics not to press every last possibility [of challenging the results]." Lately, however, both Moulitsas and Marshall have railed repeatedly about the "bogus" issue of voter fraud.

What's going on? After all its worries about Ohio in 2004—and before that, Florida in 2000—why has the Left decided that voter fraud simply doesn't exist? The short answer is: It's useful. In 2000 and 2004, charging voter fraud was a useful way to question the legitimacy of George W. Bush's presidency. Now, in 2007, denying the existence of voter fraud is a useful way to question the legitimacy of George W. Bush's presidency. If the other guys are accused of doing it, they say, it's a scandal; if we're accused of doing it, it's a fantasy.

Voter Fraud in St. Louis

The only problem is, voter fraud is a problem. It was a problem when Democrats were touting it, and it's a problem now when Democrats are denying it, and it will remain a problem in the future. Three examples from recent years are enough to prove that concerns about voter fraud are not a fantasy, but a distinct reality.

St. Louis, 2000–2001. It would be an understatement to call conditions at the polls in St. Louis chaotic during the 2000 presidential election. With voters' rolls a shambles, would-be voters crowded polling places, so much so that Democrats convinced a judge to order the polls to stay open three hours after the specified closing time. Republicans dashed to court and got another judge to order them closed after only 45 minutes' additional voting. The extension alone was not evidence of fraud, but a few months later, as the city was gearing up for a mayoral election, the *St. Louis Post-Dispatch* found that one in ten voters registered in St. Louis were also registered somewhere else. All those registrations made for some eye-popping totals. "The number of registered voters threatens to outnumber the voting age population," wrote Sen. Christopher Bond (R., Mo.) in a *Washington Post* op-ed. "A total of 247,135 St. Louis residents, dead or alive, are registered to vote compared with the City's voting-age population of 258,532. That translates to a whopping 96 percent registration rate."

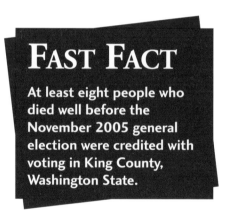

FAST FACT

At least eight people who died well before the November 2005 general election were credited with voting in King County, Washington State.

Dead People and Dogs Registered to Vote

Then there were the 3,000 voter-registration cards submitted by Democratic groups on the last day voters could register for the may-

The U.S. Senate voted to unseat Senator Ophelia Ford over questions of voter fraud in the election that won her the position.

oral primary. A number of them turned out to be for dead people. One registered voter was a dog named Ritzy. Mayor Clarence Harmon—a Democrat—told the Associated Press that voter fraud is "widespread and insidious in the body politic." "This is a little river town that's got a very bad history of very bad election fraud," Harmon said. "If we don't straighten out this fundamental issue, what's going to happen to us?"

After the election, Bond produced a thick dossier of irregularities entitled "St. Louis Election Fraud: A Primer." He blamed many of the problems on the Clinton-era "motor voter" law, which loosened requirements for voter registration. But his proposals for reform faced determined opposition from Democratic officials led by Missouri representative William Lacy Clay. In the end, a compromise was reached, with better voting machines and registration standards. But in St. Louis, the next voting scandal is only an election away.

Paying Voters to Register

South Dakota, 2002. The race between Democratic senator Tim Johnson and Republican challenger John Thune was always close, even before we learned that Johnson defeated Thune by just 524 votes. Then we learned that people were allowed to vote without identification; that out-of-state attorneys brought in by the Democratic party coached voters at the polls; and that those lawyers, in effect, engaged in illegal electioneering by setting up get-out-the-vote offices at the polls. Then there was the woman whom the state Democratic party paid $2 for each new voter she signed up on the state's Indian reservations. She made almost $13,000, much of it from suspicious signatures. She was charged with forgery, but the case fell apart when a state expert witness suggested that all the people who said their names had been signed—not one of them, not two of them, but all of them—were lying. Baffled state officials dropped the case, and it all ended in a murky mess.

Washington State, 2004. The governor's race between Democrat Christine Gregoire and Republican Dino Rossi was among the closest ever: Gregoire won by 129 votes out of 2.8 million cast. Various early counts showed Rossi winning by 261 votes, and then by 42 votes, and then, finally, the balance tipping slightly to Gregoire. A race that tight, and that important, was going to receive a lot of scrutiny, and subsequent investigations revealed lots of problems.

Deleting 55,000 Registrations

For example, in King County alone, officials found 1,800 more votes than people who had signed in at polling stations. They also found hundreds of provisional votes that were counted as regular votes. They also found dozens of examples of that old favorite, dead voters. After the controversy, state officials did a first-ever examination of the voting rolls and in 2006 announced that they had deleted 55,000 registrations.

That figure included 19,579 names of people who were dead and 35,445 otherwise illegal registrations. A little later, state officials purged another 848 names from the voting rolls—all were felons found to be illegally on lists of eligible voters.

Voter Fraud No Fantasy

St. Louis, South Dakota, and Washington State. If you want more examples you can add the phony names that were registered to vote in Ohio, the dead who voted in Milwaukee, and a long list of election tricks in Louisiana. Not all those cases resulted in criminal prosecutions. And not all the prosecutions resulted in guilty verdicts or pleas. But each case was serious enough to warrant investigation. And each revealed significant problems in the voting systems of various states. And, of course, fraud does not have to be terribly widespread to affect elections that are decided by 524 or 129 votes.

In other words, voter fraud is a real concern. It is difficult to pursue, and difficult to prove. But it's not a fantasy. Ritzy the dog could tell you that.

EVALUATING THE AUTHOR'S ARGUMENTS:

The author cites as voter fraud that voter rolls include persons who are deceased or may not be entitled to vote. Does the author tell us how many votes were supposedly cast by such persons? Does that matter in terms of proving that voter fraud is a serious problem? Why or why not?

Voter Fraud Has Been Exaggerated

Lorraine C. Minnite

"The claim that voter fraud threatens the integrity of American elections is itself a fraud."

Lorraine C. Minnite argues in the following viewpoint that voter fraud rarely occurs. Claims of fraud, when investigated, she asserts, often prove to be false or unintentional mistakes. The author says that there is a long history in America of claiming voter fraud when the base of power begins to shift from one party to another. The victims of false fraud allegations, she says, are voters struggling to be included in the political process. Minnite is assistant professor of political science at Columbia University and author of *Securing the Vote: An Analysis of Election Fraud.*

AS YOU READ, CONSIDER THE FOLLOWING QUESTIONS:

1. According to the author, how many people were convicted of or pleaded guilty to illegal voting between 2002 and 2005 on the federal level?
2. Which party, according to the author, alleged voter fraud by newly enfranchised freed black Americans during the late nineteenth century?
3. Which party, according to the author, currently is promoting baseless claims of voter fraud?

Lorraine C. Minnite, *Project Vote,* 2006. Reproduced by permission.

Voter fraud is the "intentional corruption of the electoral process by the voter." This definition covers knowingly and willingly giving false information to establish voter eligibility, and knowingly and willingly voting illegally or participating in a conspiracy to encourage illegal voting by others. All other forms of corruption of the electoral process and corruption committed by elected or election officials, candidates, party organizations, advocacy groups or campaign workers fall under the wider definition of election fraud.

Voter Fraud Is Rare

Voter fraud is extremely rare. At the federal level, records show that only 24 people were convicted of or pleaded guilty to illegal voting between 2002 and 2005, an average of eight people a year. The available state-level evidence of voter fraud, culled from interviews, reviews of newspaper coverage and court proceedings, while not definitive, is also negligible.

The lack of evidence of voter fraud is not because of a failure to codify it. It is not as if the states have failed to detail the ways voters could corrupt elections. There are hundreds of examples drawn from state election codes and constitutions that illustrate the precision with which the states have criminalized voter and election fraud. If we use the same standards for judging voter fraud crime rates as we do for other crimes, we must conclude that the lack of evidence of arrests, indictments or convictions for any of the practices defined as voter fraud means very little fraud is being committed.

Mistakes, Not Fraud

Most voter fraud allegations turn out to be something other than fraud. A review of news stories over a recent two year period found that reports of voter fraud were most often limited to local races and individual acts and fell into three categories: unsubstantiated or false claims by the loser of a close race, mischief and administrative or voter error.

> **FAST FACT**
>
> Between 2002 and 2005, only nine people were charged by the federal government with voting more than once in an election, and only five of those nine pleaded guilty or were convicted.

The more complex are the rules regulating voter registration and voting, the more likely voter mistakes, clerical errors, and the like will be wrongly identified as "fraud." Voters play a limited role in the electoral process. Where they interact with the process they confront an array of rules that can trip them up. In addition, one consequence of expanding voting opportunities, i.e. permissive absentee voting systems, is a corresponding increase in opportunities for casting unintentionally illegal ballots if administrative tracking and auditing systems are flawed.

Fraud Alleged for Partisan Advantage

There is a long history in America of elites using voter fraud allegations to restrict and shape the electorate. In the late nineteenth cen-

Democratic and Republican party observers ensure no fraud takes place during a hand count of absentee ballots that did not register on the machine counter in a South Carolina election.

tury when newly freed black Americans were swept into electoral politics, and where blacks were the majority of the electorate, it was the Democrats who were threatened by a loss of power, and it was the Democratic party that erected new rules said to be necessary to respond to alleged fraud by black voters. Today, the success of voter registration drives among minorities and low income people in recent years threatens to expand the base of the Democratic party and tip the balance of power away from the Republicans. Consequently, the use of baseless voter fraud allegations for partisan advantage has become the exclusive domain of Republican party activists.

Fraud Claims Used to Disenfranchise

The historically disenfranchised are often the target of voter fraud allegations. Fraud allegations today typically point the finger at those belonging to the same categories of voters accused of fraud in the past—the marginalized and formerly disenfranchised, urban dwellers, immigrants, blacks, and lower status voters. These populations are mostly found among those still struggling for full inclusion in American life.

Better data collection and election administration will improve the public discussion of voter fraud and lead to more appropriate policies. We need better data, better election administration, transparency and more responsible journalism to improve public understanding of the legitimate ways in which electoral outcomes can be distorted and manipulated. This will help ensure that new laws and rules to prevent fraud are narrowly targeted to solve legitimate problems rather than used as a strategy to shape the electorate for partisan advantage.

Fraud Claims Are Fraudulent

The claim that voter fraud threatens the integrity of American elections is itself a fraud. It is being used to persuade the public that deceitful and criminal voters are manipulating the electoral system. No available evidence suggests that voters are intentionally corrupting the electoral process. . . . The lack of evidence is not due to a failure to codify voter fraud as a crime, nor is it due to the inability or unwillingness of local law enforcement agencies to investigate or prosecute potential cases of voter fraud. In fact, when we probe most allegations of voter fraud we find errors, incompetence and partisanship. The exaggerated fear of voter fraud has a long history of scuttling efforts to make voting easier and more inclusive, especially for marginalized groups in American society. With renewed partisan vigor fantasies of fraud are being spun again to undo some of the progress America has made lowering barriers to the vote.

EVALUATING THE AUTHORS' ARGUMENTS:

Now that you have read this viewpoint and the preceding one, do you believe voter fraud is a serious problem? Why or why not?

Chapter 3

How Can the Election Process Be Improved?

COMMISSION *on*

FEDERAL ELECTION REFORM

JAMES A. BAKER III INSTITUTE FOR PUBLIC POLICY

CENTER *for* DEMOCRACY & ELECTION MANAGEMENT

The Carter-Baker Commission on Federal Election Reform issued a report with eighty-seven recommendations in 2005 that served as a basis for making ongoing improvements to the election process.

Voting Should Be Compulsory

J-Ro

"Compulsory voting would ensure that our government represents the will of all people, not just those who care to show up at polls."

Author J-Ro argues in the following viewpoint that voting is a civic duty that should be compulsory. The author argues that compulsory voting would result in a better-educated electorate. Campaign strategy would focus on convincing voters rather than rallying a voter base, says the author. Compulsory voting, contends the author, would give voters with less income more voice in elections. If voting is compulsory, the author says, voting laws should be changed to make voting easy. J-Ro is a musician and designer residing in Washington, D.C.

AS YOU READ, CONSIDER THE FOLLOWING QUESTIONS:

1. To what other civic duties does the author compare the duty to vote?
2. What alternative would the author provide for those compelled to vote who do not wish to support any of the candidates?
3. What penalty does the author say should be imposed on those who fail to vote?

J-Ro, "Should We Force All Americans to Vote?" *theseminal.com*, July 14, 2007. Reproduced by permission.

Voter turnout in America, especially in midterm elections, constantly hovers around 50% of the eligible voting population. Instead of being a country ruled by the majority, we are more accurately a country ruled by those who turn out at the polls. Today, 32 countries have compulsory voting laws, including some very successful ones such as Switzerland, Greece, and Australia, and you'd be hard pressed to say these countries are significantly less free or less prosperous because of it. Perhaps it is time for America to adopt the same kind of regulations? The question really is, can our government effectively represent all Americans, as it claims to, if it is elected by merely half of its citizens?

Voting Is a Civic Duty

The arguments against *compulsory voting* typically run in the rights vs. responsibilities vein. Rights like free speech are given to all Americans, but all Americans do not need to exercise their right to free speech. Coercing people to vote, so the argument goes, is a severe breach of our liberty. I don't buy this line of thinking, for two reasons. One, I think compulsory voting can be created in such a way as to allow people a real choice. Two, I believe there is some kind of civic duty to vote, and I believe we can enforce that without taking away anyone's fundamental rights. Living in America does require some responsibilities and duties in exchange for the benefits we all enjoy. Jury duty or registering for the Selective Service are the most obvious. I don't see why voting shouldn't be part of that lineup, and I don't think we are changing American philosophy drastically by making voting more of a responsibility than a waive-able right.

Inevitably when discussing compulsory voting, many non-voters bring up the point that they do not vote because no candidates are worth voting for. This is a legitimate complaint, but a compulsory voting law does not need to force people to choose between two or more candidates, only to show up and vote. There should be an option to abstain or pass on every compulsory ballot, meaning that while citizens would be required to show up, they don't actually have to support any candidates. We cannot force people to make a choice, but we can ask them to declare their non-choice officially.

Who Has Compulsory Voting?

Country	Level of Enforcement
Argentina	Weak Enforcement
Australia	Strict Enforcement
Austria (Tyrol)	Weak Enforcement
Austria (Vorarlberg)	Weak Enforcement
Belgium	Strict Enforcement
Bolivia	N/A
Brazil	Weak Enforcement
Chile	Weak Enforcement
Costa Rica	Not Enforced
Cyprus	Strict Enforcement
Dominican Republic	Weak Enforcement
Ecuador	Weak Enforcement
Egypt	N/A
Fiji	Strict Enforcement
France (Senate only)	N/A
Gabon	N/A
Greece	Weak Enforcement
Guatemala	Not Enforced
Honduras	Not Enforced
Italy	Weak/Not Enforced
Liechtenstein	Weak Enforcement
Luxembourg	Strict Enforcement
Mexico	Weak Enforcement
Nauru	Strict Enforcement
Netherlands	Not Enforced
Paraguay	N/A
Peru	Weak Enforcement
Philippines	Not Enforced
Singapore	Strict Enforcement
Switzerland (Schaffhausen)	Strict Enforcement
Thailand	Not Enforced
Turkey	Weak Enforcement
Uruguay	Strict Enforcement

Taken from: International Institute for Democracy and Electoral Assistance.

Make Voting Easier

In a similar line of thought, many argue that the cost of voting is not worth the reward. To be able to vote in America requires some kind of social and economic cost, even if that cost is low. You have to fill out forms to register to vote, you have to remember when to vote, and you have to physically go to a polling place to cast a ballot. For those who feel that their one vote is only a drop in the bucket, that they cannot influence elections and furthermore that they have no interest in any of the candidates, even this low cost of voting is too much, as the reward in their eyes is close to nothing. Though I would call these people lazy, there is validity to their core argument. Therefore, compulsory voting laws would need to be enacted in conjunction with voting access laws. Lowering the cost of voting is something we can and should do. In the best scenario, voting would be conducted online, in person, or by mail, and the voting window would be widened from 12 hours on one day to an entire week, or even an entire month. Voters would receive ballots, via the mail or electronically, automatically, and would have the option of casting their ballot sometime within the mandated voting period, using whatever method—online, by mail, or at a physical polling place—they like. At the very least, voter registration should be available online and be more or less automatic. You should be able to transfer your voter registration between states with minimal fuss, and you should be required to register when you turn 18, just like the Selective Service. By making voting easier, we should be able to lower the cost of voting to a point at which people will feel voting is worthwhile, or at the very least not unduly burdened by the process.

Fine Those Who Do Not Vote

The last argument against compulsory voting hinges on punishment. Here, I agree with naysayers in that jail time is too harsh a punishment for not voting. A small fine or community service are all that is necessary to raise the cost of defying the law and not voting to a sufficiently high level. Punishments should be light, and there must be some leniency involved for people over,

FAST FACT

In many countries with compulsory voting, it is required to vote only if you are a registered voter, but it is not compulsory to register.

say, the age of 70, Jehovah's Witnesses and other religious reasons, extenuating circumstances such as sickness, etc. . . . . It wouldn't take much in the way of punishment to raise the voter turnout rates dramatically in this country, and if people decided a fine was preferable to voting, the government could at least put their money to good use.

Compulsory Voting Would Improve Elections

The advantages of compulsory voting, however, are vast. For one, the cost of campaigning would fall. Get out the vote campaigns would no longer be necessary, and because all citizens would be required to vote, I think you can reasonably assume people would pay slightly more attention to politics, meaning media campaigns could be a bit smaller. Secondly, compulsory voting could limit the effects of money

It has been suggested that electronic voting machines could make it easier for people to participate in elections in a compulsory voting system.

and special interests on campaigns. Strategy would no longer be about rallying your base, as everyone in that base would be voting anyway, but rather about convincing voters. The poor would be more accurately represented in the electorate. Those who make less money vote less often, meaning that our elections are controlled by those with cash. Even better, with all citizens voting, everyone running for office has an interest in a well-educated electorate. Instead of voter registration drives, we would have voter education drives, hopefully elevating the political discourse in this country. Some even argue that because candidates would be more focused on swinging voters than rallying voters, they would adopt more centrist policies, thus stabilizing government. Lastly, interfering with the vote would be a lot harder and a lot less effective. Republican initiatives to disenfranchise black voters . . . would be less effective because they would have to influence so many more people to make a difference.

All Americans Would Have a Voice

Most importantly however, compulsory voting would ensure that our government represents the will of all people, not just those who care to show up at the polls. Leaders would have greater political legitimacy, voter mandates would be clearer, and because everyone has at least some kind of stake in the system, our democracy should be more stable. However, even if none of the above advantages came to pass, at the very least all Americans would have a voice, and so those who are marginalized in our system, those who are poor and underprivileged, without means or connections, would still be able to participate, at least politically, as full citizens. We may not be equals in our neighborhoods, in the job market, or in our social circles, but at least we would be equal in the eyes of the government. That is a goal worth fighting for, don't you agree?

EVALUATING THE AUTHOR'S ARGUMENTS:

The author argues that voting should be seen as a duty rather than a right. Do you agree? Give reasons for your answer.

Voting Should Not Be Compulsory

Jacob Euteneuer

> *"Compulsory voting only dumbs down and slows down elections."*

Jacob Euteneuer argues in the following viewpoint that compulsory voting will not improve elections because those who do not vote are uninformed or do not care who wins. Making uninformed voters vote, he says, will make elections less meaningful and dilute the impact of informed voters. In Australia, which has compulsory voting, he says a percentage of voters simply deface their ballots rather than cast votes for candidates. Elections will have better results, he argues, if only those truly motivated to vote cast votes. Euteneuer writes for the *Daily Nebraskan.*

AS YOU READ, CONSIDER THE FOLLOWING QUESTIONS:

1. According to the author, what percentage of Americans participate in primary elections?
2. In the author's opinion, if those who would not otherwise vote are forced to vote, what might govern their choice between candidates?
3. How many Australian voters deface their ballots?

For some reason whenever something appears to be broken, the answer always seems to be more and never less.

Such is the case with the American voting process, which while not officially broken, seems to be getting a bit rusty in the joints. For primary elections, less than 35 percent of American registered voters go to the polls and vote. Thirty-five percent of the population is effectively speaking on behalf of the other 65 percent.

Some lawmakers find this idea dissatisfying and depressing. So they have proposed the idea of mandatory, or compulsory (which sounds nicer), voting laws in which all Americans would be required to register to vote and to show up at the polling place on Election Day. But do we really want everyone in America to be voting on Election Day?

The Uninformed Do Not Vote

Americans love to vote, or more accurately, Americans love to vote about things they know about and things they care about.

Lack of participation by voters in elections prompts some to suggest implementing a system of mandatory voting.

Go on the Internet and find a poll. A video game Web site regularly has polls that over 1 million people partake in. These aren't important questions, such as should we be in Iraq or not. They are simple questions that people both understand and for some reason care about, like who would win in a fight, Mega Man or Link (Link).

Still, millions of people vote in these polls. So there is no doubt that the American people love to vote when they know what is going on. The reason there is such low voter turnout in elections, especially primaries, is because voters either do not care about the candidates or the voters do not know about the candidates.

FAST FACT

Youth voter turnout (age 18–29) was highest in 2004 in Minnesota (71 percent), Wisconsin (65 percent), Kentucky (60 percent), and Iowa (60 percent).

More Votes Does Not Mean Better Votes

The problem with mandatory voting laws is that they do not teach you, they merely force you into action. And just because our president thinks decisive action is the best of all worlds, that does not mean the American people think that.

Australia is one of the few democracies in the world to actually have a compulsory voting law in place. The people of Australia generally come out and vote in numbers that would make Americans blush. In their last federal election, 95 percent of registered voters turned up at the polls. At the 2004 federal election, 67 percent of Americans decided to take the time out of their busy days to decide who would be running the Earth's only superpower. Would an extra 28 percent of the populace come out and vote if they were subjected to a $15 fine, as they would be in Australia? Most likely they would, but whom would they be voting for and why?

Political scientists generally say compulsory voting laws increase the amount of liberal votes by 2 to 3 percent. This is largely because poor and disillusioned minorities would side with the liberal cause over the conservative.

However, someone who is forced to vote in an election who otherwise would not have voted will probably just vote for whoever the hell has the coolest sounding last name (Buttz in '08!).

Some Do Not Want to Vote

In Australia there exists something called the "donkey vote." No, this isn't a vote for the Democrats, it is when someone who is forced to show up and vote just scribbles and defaces their ballot and drops it in the box. According to Slate.com, there were 500,000 of these votes in the last Australian election. Keep in mind that Australia is only forcing 10 million people to the polls every election day. One out of every 20 Australians took the time to go down to the polls and write obscene words on their ballot.

Now this isn't against the law—compulsory voting laws just say you have to show up to the polls—but it is completely idiotic. These people obviously do not want to vote. They obviously know little of the political world, but yet they are forced to drive down to the polling place and write "POOP" in big letters with black pen on their ballot. One would think that the result in America would be even worse, because, as Americans, we love our freedom.

The Australians appear to be a bit wishy-washy over the issue. The Australian government Web site says about compulsory voting that

Voter Turnout in the United States

U.S. Voter Turnout Statistics, 2006, 2002, 1994	Young People 18 to 29	Adults 30 and over
2006		
Number of Citizens Eligible to Vote in 2006	41.9 million	158.2 million
2002		
Number of Votes Cast	8.9 million	78.9 million
Citizen Voter Turnout Rate	22 percent	52 percent
Share of all Voters	10 percent	90 percent
1994		
Number of Votes Cast	10.4 million	75.2 million
Citizen Voter Turnout Rate	26 percent	55 percent
Share of all Voters	12 percent	88 percent

Taken from: The Center for Information and Research on Civic Learning and Engagement.

it is "undemocratic to force people to vote—an infringement on liberty." You really do not need to say much more than that. Why is Bush not jumping on this one and removing Australian Prime Minister John Howard from power and freeing the Australian people (the answer to this one is of course because Australia has very little oil deposits.)? The point is that the American people will not have the will of others forced upon them.

Dumbing Down Elections

In the end Americans' resistance to being forced to do anything is a blessing. It prevents laws such as compulsory voting from passing. Compulsory voting only dumbs down and slows down elections. By watering down the entire voting pool, it prevents voters who are well educated and well thought out from having any conceivable effect on the outcome of the election.

Compulsory voting should not take place in America because unoriginal and boring people will lose one of their favorite phrases. They would have to amend it to be, "The only things you have to do in life are die, pay taxes and vote, unless you have a spare $15 lying around to pay the fine." Honestly, that just doesn't have the same ring to it.

EVALUATING THE AUTHORS' ARGUMENTS:

Now that you have read this viewpoint and the one preceding it, do you think Americans, if forced to vote, would think seriously about the choices or, as this author suggests, deface their ballots or vote for the "coolest name"? Give reasons for your opinion.

Viewpoint 3

Instant Runoff Voting Would Improve Elections

"IRV . . . not only allows voters to voice their real preferences; it also ensures that the will of the true majority, not a mere plurality, produces the winner."

David Cobb, Patrick Barrett, and Caleb Kleppner

David Cobb, Patrick Barrett, and Caleb Kleppner argue in the following viewpoint that instant runoff voting (IRV), in which voters rank the candidates rather than voting only for one, will give more choice and prevent election of candidates opposed by a majority of voters. IRV, they argue, also will reduce negative campaigning targeting independent and third-party candidates. IRV, they contend, will increase competition among candidates and voter participation. Cobb and Barrett are fellows of the Liberty Tree Foundation for the Democratic Revolution and Kleppner is a partner in Electronic Solutions.

AS YOU READ, CONSIDER THE FOLLOWING QUESTIONS:

1. Among industrialized nations, according to the authors, only what three use plurality voting?
2. What is the downside, in the authors' view, to holding a runoff election?
3. What U.S. city has used IRV for all local elections since 2004?

David Cobb, Patrick Barrett, Caleb Kleppner, "Preserving and Expanding the Right to Vote: Ranked-Choice Voting," *Advance*, July 6, 2006, pp. 109–113. Reproduced by permission of the publisher and the authors. Patrick Barrett and David Cobb are fellows with the Democratic Elections Program of the Liberty Tree Foundation for the Democratic Revolution. For more information, go to www.libertytreefdr.org.

T he most widely used electoral system in the United States, plurality voting, also known as first past the post (FPTP), is also the most archaic and least democratic. Voters choose one candidate, and the candidate with the most votes is elected, even if she receives less than a majority. Although the system is simple and it seems fair to elect the candidate with the most votes, it suffers from a variety of flaws. As a result of these flaws, most countries in the world have abandoned plurality voting. Among industrial democracies, only the US, Canada and the UK still use plurality voting for national elections.

Flaws of Plurality Elections

The flaws of plurality elections stem from the possibility of electing a candidate that a majority of voters oppose, thereby violating the principle of majority rule and leaving most people without representation. This occurs when the majority splits its votes between two candidates, allowing a third candidate with less overall support (and often strongly disliked by the majority) to win. Typically, this happens when a strong third party or independent runs in a race in which the Democratic and Republican candidates are competitive, but it also happens in primaries when multiple candidates target the same voters. . . .

Furthermore, when a candidate wins office with less than a majority of the vote, even if that candidate is preferred by an actual majority, that candidate is likely to enter office with a weak or unclear mandate. For example, when Bill Clinton won office in 1992 with 43% of the vote, Senate Majority Leader Bob Dole vowed to represent the majority of Americans who did not vote for Clinton by filibustering [trying to block legislation by making long speeches] Clinton's policy proposals and forcing Clinton to gain 60 senate votes to override the filibuster.

Plurality Not Representative

In addition, plurality elections are unrepresentative and in fact create disincentives for voters to vote for their favorite candidate. If your favorite candidate is not among the frontrunners, your options are not great. You can cast a symbolic vote for a loser who will likely be ignored by the media or blamed as a spoiler who caused the election of her supporters' least favorite candidate. Or you can hold your nose and settle for a lesser evil to avoid a greater evil. Or you can choose not to vote at all, which has become the option of the majority. The problem is that plurality elections give many voters an incentive not to vote for their favorite candidate, which means that the election is not an accurate measure of whom the people want in office and thus leaves many if not most of them unrepresented and turned off to the electoral process. . . .

Marginalizing Third Party Candidates

Finally, plurality voting skews media coverage and encourages negative campaigning. Because voters have an incentive not to consider third party and independent candidates, media outlets tend to ignore them and the issues they are trying to raise. Instead, media focus on polling results, fundraising and personalities rather than substantive policy issues. Mudslinging is not very effective when voters can support a candidate other than the slinger and the target of the mud. Since plurality voting marginalizes independent and third party candidates as irrelevant or spoilers, negative campaigning is more widespread under plurality rather than other voting methods.

Runoff Help

Runoffs represent a real improvement over plurality elections, but they do not entirely overcome the shortcomings of plurality elections, and they have problems of their own. Runoff elections ensure majority rule of those who participate in the runoff, but turnout varies greatly between the two rounds. For example, turnout dropped in 98% of all federal

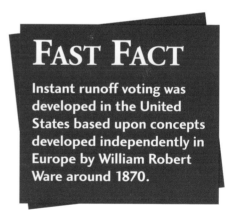

FAST FACT

Instant runoff voting was developed in the United States based upon concepts developed independently in Europe by William Robert Ware around 1870.

runoffs between 1994 and 2004. Aggregate turnout in all of these runoffs was 36% lower than in the first round. This drop in turnout undermines majority rule. Also, the two candidates advancing to a runoff can receive together less than 50% of the vote, meaning that a majority of voters did not vote for someone in the runoff. In addition, runoffs

Who Uses IRV in the United States?

U.S. governments currently using IRV:

San Francisco, CA
Burlington, VT
Takoma Park, MD
Louisiana
South Carolina
Arkansas
North Carolina

U.S. governments working on IRV implementation:

Minneapolis, MN
Oakland, CA
Pierce County, WA
Berkeley, CA
Ferndale, MI

U.S. governments with an IRV option:

Vancouver, WA
Santa Clara County, CA
San Leandro, CA

Ann Arbor (MI), New York (NY), and Yonkers (NY) have used IRV in the past.

Taken from: FairVote.org. www.fairvote.org/index.php?page=1960.

reduce but do not eliminate the spoiler problem, especially when several similar candidates are competing for the same runoff spot, perhaps against an incumbent. Those candidates can split the vote, allowing another candidate with less overall support to gain a spot in the runoff.

But perhaps the biggest downside of a runoff is the burden of holding a second election. This burden falls mainly on taxpayers, who pay for the election, and on election officials and poll workers, but it also falls on candidates, campaign workers, and, importantly, campaign contributors. Since runoffs generally occur soon after the initial election, they give advantages to candidates who can raise money quickly from large donors, further exacerbating disparities in campaign finance between candidates. Lastly, for those who participate in an election, it takes time away from work and family and forces people to sift through campaign mailers, phone calls and advertisements.

Head-to-head runoffs also encourage vicious negative campaigning since voters cannot escape from the two candidates slinging mud to support another one. This is one reason that voter turnout generally drops in a runoff.

IRV Is the Solution

There is a tested and proven solution to these problems. . . . It was used in public elections as early as 1897 in Australia, in state-wide primaries in the United States in the teens and 20s of the last century, in local elections from the 1930s to the 1950s, for all local elections in San Francisco since 2004, for mayor of Burlington, Vermont since 2006, and for overseas military voters in Arkansas, Louisiana and South Carolina. In recent years, legislation requiring or allowing this method has been adopted in Takoma Park, MD; Ferndale, MI; Santa Clara County, CA; Oakland, CA; Berkeley, CA; and Vancouver, WA, and it is likely to be on the ballot in Minneapolis, MN, in November 2006.

It depends on a simple but powerful idea: allow voters to rank candidates in order of choice and then use those rankings to elect the candidates preferred by a majority of voters. In essence, by allowing voters to rank candidates, it allows voters to simultaneously participate in an election and a runoff. The system is called instant runoff voting (IRV) or ranked-choice voting (RCV).

Eliminating the Spoiler Effect

Unlike plurality voting, which pressures voters to reject their preferred candidate in favor of a "lesser evil" who *may* have a better chance of defeating the candidate they most fear, IRV allows them to choose both. In this way, it eliminates the so-called "spoiler effect" and "wasted vote" phenomenon and gives voters a more democratic set of choices. Under IRV, voters simply rank candidates in order of their preference (first, second, etc.). If a candidate wins a majority of first choice votes, that candidate is the winner. If no candidate gets a majority of first choices, the rankings are used to perform a series of runoff rounds. In each round, the lowest vote-getting candidate is eliminated, and

The city election director of Burlington, Vermont, holds a runoff election ballot for the mayor's race.

each ballot is recounted for the voter's most preferred candidate who is still in the race. Candidates are successively eliminated until one candidate receives a majority. IRV therefore not only allows voters to voice their real preferences; it also ensures that the will of the true majority, not a mere plurality, produces the winner of each election.

By ranking candidates, the voter is saying, "I want to vote for my first choice candidate, and if she/he makes the runoff, I want my vote to stay with my favorite candidate. But if my favorite candidate doesn't make the runoff, I want my vote to go to someone who has a chance of defeating the candidate I most fear and oppose."

IRV is much like convention style voting, which is recommended in *Robert's Rules* [*Robert's Rules of Order* is a book of rules used for running meetings fairly]: everyone votes for a candidate, the candidate with the fewest votes is eliminated, and everyone votes again for a candidate. With IRV, you declare your vote in every round by simply ranking the candidates. Your ballot will support in every round your favorite candidate who is still in the race.

Benefits of IRV

In the short-term, IRV would have several beneficial effects on the electoral process. It would give voters more choice, both in terms of an ability to express themselves and in terms of the menu of candidates to choose from. It would free major party candidates from the fear that an independent or third party candidate would spoil their election, which means that major parties could work constructively with minor parties on the issues they agree on. IRV would ensure that the will of the majority is respected, which would strengthen the mandate of candidates winning office.

IRV would also have positive effects on candidates and campaigns. A wider range of candidates would be freed to compete in both primary and general elections, and this would encourage new candidates to enter the ring. This would likely increase the diversity of candidates, especially bringing more young people, working class people, women, and people of color into the process. These candidates may well appeal to groups of voters who are increasingly dropping out of the process, and over time, this would likely slow or reverse the trend of declining participation. It would also increase the competition among candidates and elected officials and thereby increase the power of voters to hold them accountable.

Finally, in a multi-candidate race, there is less incentive to use negative campaigning. Most instant runoff elections would still boil down to a race between a Democrat and a Republican, at least in partisan races, so those candidates will have to continue to differentiate themselves and even attack each other, but they will not feel the pressure to bash the independent and minor party candidates with whom they have the most agreement.

EVALUATING THE AUTHORS' ARGUMENTS:

Do you agree with the authors that more choice in elections is a good thing? Could more choice ever be a bad thing? Give reasons for your answers.

Instant Runoff Voting Would Harm Elections

Minnesota Voters Alliance

"IRV should be opposed by anyone who values true democracy!"

The Minnesota Voters Alliance argues in the following viewpoint that replacing primaries with Instant Runoff Voting (IRV) will hurt elections. IRV, the authors say, would suppress minority views and reduce voter turnout. Primaries, say the authors, narrow the candidates, resulting in more post-primary debate, which benefits voters. The authors contend that IRV would create a multiplicity of candidates, confusing voters. Minnesota Voters Alliance is a citizens group active in election issues.

AS YOU READ, CONSIDER THE FOLLOWING QUESTIONS:
1. If IRV were used in the 2008 presidential election, in the authors' view, how many candidates would there likely be?
2. In what elections do the authors contend the key issues are first identified and examined?
3. If IRV became the norm, how do the authors say that could affect the nature of the two-party system?

Minnesota Voters Alliance, "Instant Runoff Elections," 2006. Reproduced by permission.

What is it? IRV, using just one election with no primary, requires voters to rank candidates in order of preference. If no candidate receives greater than 50% of the vote, the candidate with the least number of first-choice votes is eliminated and the second-choice votes on those ballots are transferred to the remaining candidates. The process is repeated until a 50% + 1 majority is achieved.

IRV should be opposed by anyone who values true democracy! The push to implement such elections (nation-wide) was started by a largely partisan group for the main purpose of minimizing the spoiler effect of third parties, with total disregard of the negative consequences on the electorate. The following list of arguments was taken from "Better Ballot Campaign," a front group for FairVoteMN.org, which promotes IRV. Our analysis of each argument [appears after each argument]. We believe that none of their arguments hold water. *You* be the judge! . . .

There Is No Majority Winner Requirement
Proponents say that the current primary system is flawed because [it] undermines the 50% + 1 majority-winner requirement.

Our response—There is no such thing as a majority-winner requirement! The Founders gave us a Constitutional Republic, not a majority-rule Democracy, because they knew pure majority rule often leads to tyranny.

IRV won't solve this perceived "flaw" anyway. It merely creates an illusion of a majority (and a false mandate). Once 2nd & 3rd choices are tallied (because nobody got a majority of first choices) the winner has only an artificially fabricated majority.

Additionally, the more candidates there are in an IRV race, the more difficult it will be for voters to gain knowledge of the various candidates and the more diluted the rankings will become.

In the 2001 Minneapolis mayoral race there were 22 (mostly unknown) candidates in the primary! If this had been IRV using just one election, it would have been virtually impossible for (most) voters to truly identify each of the candidates and legitimately rank their choices.

If the 2008 Presidential election were to use IRV, there could easily be 30 or more candidates in the election! Who, in their right mind, would think this is a good idea? This would be not even close to practical; and, it's the voters who pay the price.

If people don't know who they're voting for, the results can't possibly be an accurate reflection of their will. Thus, any claims of a true majority victory would have to be considered false and misleading.

Ironically, IRV does not guarantee a majority will even be elected. If no majority is produced after all rankings are tallied, the plurality winner (the one with the most votes) is declared the winner!

IRV Undermines Primaries

[IRV proponents claim primaries] weed out candidates who could win in a high-turnout general election.

Our response—This argument is conveniently directed at "nonpartisan elections" in which primaries have become almost meaningless. However, rather than being an argument in favor of Instant Runoffs, it's actually a good argument against nonpartisan elections.

The purpose of primaries (ideally suited to partisan "basis" elections) is not merely to find someone who can win, but to allow voters to "select" candidates to represent their views in the general election, to force them to prove they are worthy to serve, and to reduce the field of candidates to a more practical number.

Primaries are where key issues are identified and examined. They provide an organized environment for debate and have proven to be essential to Democracy. Eliminating them will further weaken the electoral process.

[IRV proponents claim primaries] limit post-primary political debate [by narrowing the field of candidates].

Our response—A narrower candidate field (all other things being equal) would lead to more post-primary debate, not less, and make it easier for voters to identify candidates and the issues.

FAST FACT

San Francisco spent $1.87 per registered voter on IRV voter education and also held seven hundred outreach events.

IRV could easily create a huge candidate field and turn elections into name recognition contests, virtually eliminating any chance for meaningful debate.

IRV Ballots May Be Confusing

Voters in Burlington, Vermont, IRV Mayoral Election Who Found IRV Ballots Confusing, by Educational Level:

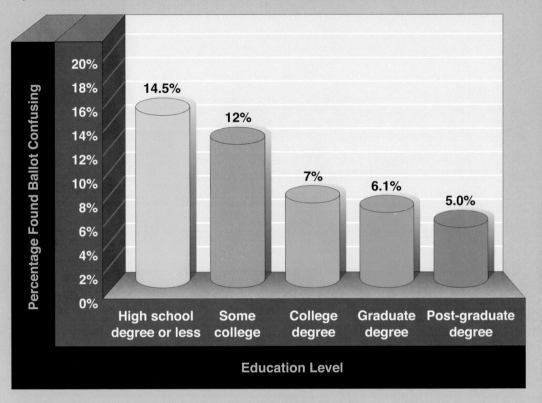

Taken from: University of Vermont study, 2006. www.uvm.edu/~vlrs/doc/IRV.pdf.

Note: The fact that third parties aren't always included in debates is a separate problem which can't be solved by IRV.

IRV Will Hurt Elections

Proponents say that IRV elections are better because they . . .

eliminate low-turnout primaries and bring the most voters together with the most candidates to choose from at the same election.

Our response—Where does it say that low primary turnout is a bad thing? Those who show up decide who the candidates are. If people don't show up, it must mean it's not that important to them, and that's their right, too.

IRV will likely produce less voter participation rather than more, especially among those who feel under-represented, once the novelty wears off and the public begins to realize that their votes carry even less weight. IRV is also more likely to deter many serious candidates who would otherwise run but lack the necessary name recognition to overcome the activist factions who have stacked the deck against them.

In the end, IRV will cause more elections to be decided by otherwise disengaged voters rallied by last minute "get-out-the-vote" campaigns.

[IRV proponents say IRV] *"empowers them to vote sincerely without being concerned about wasting their vote."*

Our response—The concept of "wasted votes" is simply ridiculous! If voters feel they are "wasting" their vote, it means they don't like any of the candidates—therefore, a ranking scheme like IRV won't solve anything, except to deny voters an important voice of dissent.

Whether voting for a favorite candidate that best represents their views or casting a legitimate vote of protest, voters have a right to "vote sincerely" for any candidate as they see fit, or none at all, if they choose to protest.

Note: Our Constitution guarantees the right to vote, but NOT the right to cast a bunch of **"just in case my candidate loses"** votes.

[IRV Proponents say IRV will] *"eliminate the cost of the primary elections."*

Our response—The government is obligated to hold elections and cost is not a valid constitutional argument to eliminate an election, i.e. a primary.

Our fight to select our candidates and our representatives at all levels of government is one of the cornerstones of our democracy, **if it's a little more costly . . . it's well worth it!** . . .

IRV Does Not Reduce Polarization

[IRV proponents claim IRV will] *"invigorate campaigns and reduce polarization by bringing multiple viewpoints into the debate and promote positive, issue based campaigns."*

Our response—How does IRV "invigorate campaigns"? It doesn't, it suppresses them. The phrase "reduces polarization by bringing in multiple viewpoints" sounds good, but it's actually meaningless rhetoric.

Since IRV provides a poor format for healthy debates in the first place, having multiple viewpoints doesn't do much good. Besides, the current Minneapolis nonpartisan elections frequently see two Democrats in the general election and polarization can't be reduced much further than that.

In 2007 the Vermont House of Representatives approved the use of runoff voting in state congressional elections.

And, why is it such a good idea to reduce polarization anyway? It's not! As Jefferson said, *"In every **free and deliberating society**, there must, from the nature of man, be opposite parties, and violent dissensions and discords."*

IRV does no more to ensure that candidates will run on the issues than any other election format. In fact, it does less. Once candidates see that the way to get elected is simply to appeal to as many voters as possible, they will be more inclined to pander rather than to persuade which will lead to popularity contests, rather than strong and open, issue-based campaigns.

In an increasingly diverse political environment, a plurality system, (where the candidate who receives the **most votes** wins, even if it's less than 50%) is far superior to one that creates only an artificial majority. If we want "3rd" parties, we should embrace pluralities.

IRV Hurts Minorities

If IRV became the norm, we could easily end up with a **"one party"** system made up of a tyrannical "ruling elite" because schemes like IRV decrease the competitiveness of the election process and put the minority at an immediate disadvantage while favoring the majority and its activist factions.

IRV serves only to suppress viewpoints (especially the minority), limit accountability by diminishing party influence, create more opportunities for irregularities and manipulation, and further **disenfranchise voters by removing them one more step away from the electoral process. . . .**

More Error with IRV

Despite the optimistic claims of IRV success, these stories paint quite a different picture: San Francisco, Vermont, Scotland. The latest news from San Francisco is that their vote-counting machines were not certified and the rankings will have to be counted and transferred by hand! This practically guarantees a high rate of error, further eroding confidence in the system. The voters in Raleigh,

NC got lucky when their City Council members flatly rejected IRV in the first place.

All in all, IRV is a terrible idea. If we want to improve our election process and the voter's confidence in it, we should support measures that will empower the citizens, not professional politicians and the bureaucracies they wish to control.

EVALUATING THE AUTHORS' ARGUMENTS:

After reading this viewpoint and the preceding one, do you think IRV will give more choice and control to voters or only create confusion? Give reasons for your answers.

Third Parties Should Be Encouraged

Joel S. Hirschhorn

Joel S. Hirschhorn argues in the following viewpoint that two-party rule suppresses meaningful choices for voters. The Republican and Democratic parties, he says, work to deny third parties access to television debates and create rules that make it difficult for third parties to get on ballots. Third-party choices, he argues, allow voters to vote their conscience rather than choose the lesser of two evils. Hirschhorn is the author of *Delusional Democracy: Fixing the Republic Without Overthrowing the Government.*

"Two-party rule has 'spoiled' our democracy."

AS YOU READ, CONSIDER THE FOLLOWING QUESTIONS:

1. What is a reason, in the author's view, that 60 percent of eligible voters did not vote in 2006?
2. How does the author believe a third party can achieve political victory?
3. How can third parties affect voter turnout, in the author's opinion?

Joel S. Hirschhorn, "Third Parties Fight for American Democracy," *populistamerica.com*, November 22, 2006. Reproduced by permission of the author.

A great democracy offers citizens sharp political choices. That's what gives political freedom meaning. With two-party control of America's political system, political options and discourse are stifled. We badly need more visible third parties that can fully participate and reach the public with information about their platforms and candidates. In a nation that so worships competition it is hypocritical that there is so little political competition.

In truth, the Democratic-Republican partnership opposes competition. They have convinced Americans that votes for third party candidates are "wasted." Yet the biggest wasted vote is for a Democrat or Republican that is almost certain to win or lose, and takes your vote for granted. [In 2006], even in the face of enormous public dissatisfaction with the two major parties, and a widespread belief that both are hopelessly corrupted by big money from corporate and other special interests, too many voters sheepishly picked from column D or R, even for sure winners or losers.

Lesser-Evil Candidates

In this remarkable year [2006] of attention to many hot issues, especially political corruption and the Iraq war, voter turnout was just over 40 percent, no better than the previous midterm election. One valid view of why 60 percent of eligible voters did not vote is that they saw little difference between the two major parties and, therefore, that their votes do not matter. It's "they're all a bunch of crooks and liars" belief, bolstered this year with so much evidence of crooks in congress and liars in the Bush administration. Where supporters of Republicans or Democrats see different positions on issues, cynical citizens see nothing but campaign propaganda and civic distraction through divisive issues. So they do not vote their conscience or for lesser-evil candidates. Most have too little information about third party candidates to vote for them.

The untold statistical story is that a minor party could achieve political victory if half of the huge block of nonvoters chose its candidates, because major party winners typically have just a little more than half of the smaller voting block.

Suppressing Third Parties

The Democratic and Republican Parties take no chances. They have used their muscle to keep third party candidates out of public

A third-party candidate for a Maryland Senate seat participates in a political debate with his Democrat and Republican opponents.

campaign venues, notably televised debates, and to create rules that make it difficult for them to get on ballots. As Tom Knapp correctly observed: "Major party candidates are cowards. They don't want to take stands that might cost them votes, but they don't want to be publicly outed as the walking blobs of Silly Putty they are, either. So, they erect difficult ballot access barriers to keep third party candidates out altogether, and when that fails they collude with their fellow Silly Puttians to, as best possible, exclude their third party opponents from the public discussion."

The two-party duopoly prefers lesser-evil voters, people considered as independents, moderates or swing voters that can be influenced by aggressive and generally misleading advertising to choose the least worse Republican or Democratic candidates. Nor do the two majors really want a large voter turnout across the entire spectrum of political views. They prefer to have well defined niche categories of voters that they can target.

Vote Conscience with Third Party

Here is a wonderful perspective about third parties by Rick Gaber: "They give the otherwise ignored, used, abused, betrayed, disgusted, disappointed, frustrated, victimized, insulted, and/or outraged voter a chance to cast a vote without feeling dirty afterwards, a reason to go to the polls at all in the first place, and maybe even to come out of the voting booth feeling great!"

In contrast to lesser-evil voters—third party voters proudly vote their conscience. They know that the odds are totally against their choices winning. Yet they do not stay home. They are true believers in American democracy. Their votes are strong messages. They are more strategic voters with long-term hopefulness about political reform, as compared to tactical lesser-evil voters hoping against reality that when the two-party pendulum swings to the other side something really good happens.

Third Parties Affect Elections

The 2006 midterm elections showed the importance of votes for third party candidates who keep fighting for a place in the American political system, despite being intentionally disadvantaged by very little money and media coverage.

Consider the Democratic majority in the Senate. Votes for third party candidates in three states were critical. Much media attention went to Democrat Jim Webb's win in Virginia by a relatively small number of votes, less than 9,000. As always, the media drummed up business by creating visions of a tight race between the two major party candidates, and ignored the third party candidate Gail Parker of the Independent Grassroots Party. As an independent fiscal conservative she received over three times the number of votes that gave Webb the victory over Republican George Allen. If just over one-third

FAST FACT

The Libertarian Party is the third-largest political party in America with more than two hundred thousand registered voters.

of those conservative voters had voted for Allen, the Democrats would not have a Senate majority. As elsewhere, some conservative voters rebelled against the Republican Party.

The Montana senate race was also featured. Democrat Jim Tester won over Republican Conrad Burns with less than a 3,000 vote margin. The

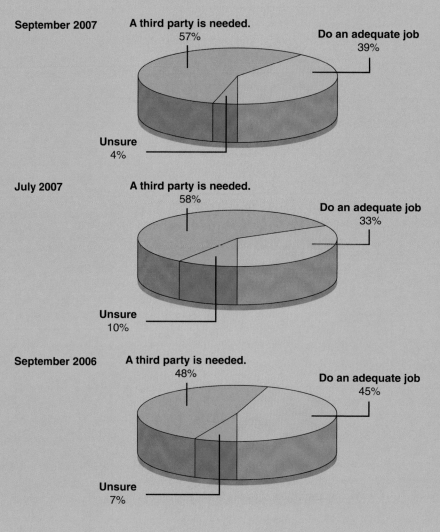

Americans Want a Third Party

In your view, do the Republican and Democratic parties do an adequate job of representing the American people, or do they do such a poor job that a third major party is needed?

September 2007

A third party is needed. 57%

Do an adequate job 39%

Unsure 4%

July 2007

A third party is needed. 58%

Do an adequate job 33%

Unsure 10%

September 2006

A third party is needed. 48%

Do an adequate job 45%

Unsure 7%

Taken from: Gallup/USA Today, October 2007.

Libertarian Party candidate, Stan Jones, received over three times that margin. So, if about one-third of those voters had gone Republican, the Democrats would not have a Senate majority. Generally, Libertarian candidates take votes away from Republicans, and certainly that was justified this year.

In Missouri, Democrat Claire McCaskill beat Republican Jim Talent with a margin of about 46,000 votes. Frank Gilmour from the Libertarian Party received more than that. He and Lydia Lewis from the Progressive Party of Missouri received some 66,000 votes. So, if two-thirds of those voters had gone Republican, the Democrats would not have a Senate majority.

Send a Message

Frank Gilmour said this about his candidacy: "For far too long, our votes have been taken for granted; we either vote for the lesser of the two evils or we do not vote at all. My candidacy offers you a choice other than the two main parties. I'm not on the extreme left or the extreme right. I live in the middle, and I believe that most of you feel the same way. Our politicians give us partisan bickering instead of legitimate debate. If you vote for me it will send a message to the two main parties that enough is enough!"

Democrats owe a lot to those third party candidates and voters in those three states. Republicans deserved what they got.

Not Just Spoilers

These three cases, as in many other races in previous years, demonstrate that votes for third party candidates are not "wasted." Nor should such candidates be falsely labeled as "spoilers." The implication is that they intentionally want to toss the race to one of the major party candidates. In truth, third party candidates believe in their mission to raise things neglected by the major parties. They can attract people that would not otherwise vote. They add integrity to our democracy. If anything, their current underdog status provides a constant reminder of just how unfair the political playing field is. They are not the problem. Our status quo political system is the problem, because two-party rule has "spoiled" our democracy.

Libertarian candidate Garrett Michael Hayes smartly put down the spoiler accusation this way; "I'm in this to win. Whether or not that's a realistic goal, I don't care. This country was founded by people whose goals sounded unrealistic at first.". . .

The time is long overdue for Americans to stop voting for candidates that can win, and start voting for those that should win. What lesser-evil voting has produced is entrenched two-party evil. We can do better. If we open our political marketplace to more competition.

EVALUATING THE AUTHOR'S ARGUMENTS:

The author responds to critics who say a vote for a third party is "wasted," by saying that the biggest wasted vote is for a Republican or Democrat that is almost certain to win or lose. Do you agree with this argument? Give reasons for your answer.

Third Parties Should Not Be Encouraged

The Prometheus Institute

"America will never see a third party achieve long-term success."

The Prometheus Institute argues in the following viewpoint that third parties are harmful. The author claims that third parties breed polarization, which can lead to legislative deadlock. Third parties, it is argued, must take extremist positions to be noticed and therefore will never appeal to a large number of voters. Third parties are not necessary to promote movements for change, and when third parties promote good ideas then eventually, says the author, one or both of the main parties will adopt those ideas, making the third party unnecessary. The Prometheus Institute is a think tank based in Orange County, California.

AS YOU READ, CONSIDER THE FOLLOWING QUESTIONS:

1. The author cites, in support of the argument that multiparty systems breed polarization, the experience of countries located in what part of the world?
2. What does the author say is the main advantage of the two-party system?
3. According to the author, Ronald Regan was elected in 1980 running on a platform almost identical to the editorial positions in what magazine?

The Prometheus Institute, "Two Is Enough," 2007. Reproduced by permission.

In the plurality system, the difficulty of gaining the requisite 51% to win generally allows only two parties to develop as legitimate political players. Everything else is just throwing away a vote.

It is for this reason, and not the fault of corporations, lobbyists, unions or politicians, that America will never see a third party achieve long-term success. Certainly, resurgent parties can become so large that they push out one of the two existing major parties, as the Republicans did in the 19th century. But such a situation is highly unlikely today, and they will never last in third-party opposition.

Third Parties Breed Polarization

It is tempting for many readers to observe the futility of third party success under the American plurality system and clamor for America to implement a proportional representation system. Some even clamor for this in public discussion. However, this would be inappropriate, in addition to being unconstitutional, for several reasons.

First, third parties breed polarization. In Western Europe, where multi-party systems are the norm, neofascist parties, communist parties, ethnic parties and separatist parties not only exist, but win seats in legislatures. Once there, they generally waste valuable public resources by soiling the legislative process with their misguided idealism in the pursuit of discredited ideologies. When they are not casting protest votes and engaging in other such exercises in uselessness, they are abandoning their principles to form strategic alliances, merely to gain power. Their lasting impact is obviously harmful, and bad enough in the generally homogenous and relatively small countries of Europe. Were proportional representation introduced in the highly diverse, gigantic melting pot of America, however, the results would be disastrous.

In Europe, votes are cast for, and seats are won by, a myriad of parties dedicated to minority interests—even single-issue parties. Imagine the American voting blocs who could form successful political parties, simply by their ability to garner a mere 5% of the vote in elections and thus win seats in Congress. The NAACP, Greenpeace, teachers unions, AFL-CIO, NOW, AARP, and the NRA immediately come to mind, and the full list is enormous. Blacks, Native Americans and Hispanics would certainly form at least one party each to represent their ethnic interests, which they feel are well-worth the heavy hand of the US government. The Religious Right would have a party in order to institutionalize its theocracy, as would the Catholic Church for perhaps different reasons. It is not far-fetched to imagine that large and politically unique states like California or Texas would form local-interest national parties, as well, *ad infinitum*. Needless to say, this is something no American wants, especially those who claim to dislike the political power of special interests.

It is understandable to express regret at the bilateral polarization of American politics. But it is certainly better than multilateral

Major Third-Party Presidential Challenges, 1832–2004

Year	Party	Candidate	Percent of Popular Vote	Number of Electoral Votes
1832	Anti-Masonic	William Wirt	7.8%	7
1848	Free Soil	Martin Van Buren	10.1%	0
1856	Whig-American	Millard Fillmore	21.5%	8
1860	Southern Democrat	John C. Breckinridge	18.1%	72
1860	Constitutional Union	John Bell	12.6%	39
1892	Populist	James B. Weaver	8.5%	22
1912	Progressive	Teddy Roosevelt	27.5%	88
1912	Socialist	Eugene V. Debbs	6.0%	0
1924	Progressive	Robert M. LaFollette	16.6%	13
1948	States' Rights	Strom Thurmond	2.4%	39
1948	Progressive	Henry Wallace	2.4%	0
1968	American Independent	George Wallace	13.5%	46
1980	Independent	John Anderson	6.6%	0
1992	Reform	H. Ross Perot	18.9%	0
1996	Reform	H. Ross Perot	8.4%	0
2000	Reform	Ralph Nader	2.7%	0
2004	Green	Ralph Nader	1.0%	0

Taken from: ThisNation.com.

polarization, where nearly *nothing* would be able to be achieved. Gridlock would be epic, as the interest groups would themselves become the parties. Thank the framers of the Constitution for saving us from this potential mess.

It is also ironic that those who find the current state of political affairs disgusting are the ones who clamor for third parties. Yes, the two parties are full of dirty opportunists. So why would you want more or them?

Third Parties Are Extremist

Libertarianism, the political position forwarded by this fine organization [The Prometheus Institute], is in good political shape. The percentage of the public identifying itself as libertarian (calling themselves "socially liberal and fiscally conservative") is up to 20%, now barely trailing liberals (24%) and conservatives (27%). Libertarian support is highest among well-educated voters, yet is still spread evenly across

Some people feel that third parties, like the Green Party, are too extreme to be accepted by mainstream voters.

demographic groups. During the 2004 election, 17 million Kerry voters didn't agree that government should do more to solve the country's problems, and 28 million Bush voters supported gay marriage. Most of these voters are likely libertarians who are frustrated with their lack of alternatives.

Despite this potential support, the Libertarian Party [LP] achieves nothing close to electoral success. Why? Despite the aforementioned institutional obstacles, the LP's general philosophy still enjoys widespread popularity. It's close enough to overtake the liberals (the Democratic Party position) and conservatives (the Republican Party position) in popularity. So why do they still fail to even win 2% of the vote? Shouldn't they at least be pulling 10–20%?

The answer is because they, like most third parties, tend toward extreme positions. The reason for this is simple. If they don't offer a stark alternative to the GOP or Democrats, they offer little appeal. Why would anyone risk wasting a vote for an unproven third party loser whose policies aren't substantially different than a proven major party? . . .

The Main Parties Pander to Third Parties

So what happens to new political movements, if they can't form third parties? Easy. In the US, they just end up being adopted by one (or sometimes both) of the two major parties. This is the main advantage of the two party system—in the long run, neither party stands for anything.

The Republicans went from the most popular party among blacks to being called plantation owners by blacks; they went from being anti-big business Progressives to being pro-corporate interests; and they went from the party of limited government to the party of interventionism and moralist legislation. The Democrats went from the party of racist Southern slaveowners and Jim Crow aficionados to affirmative-action and quota-loving race-baiters; they went from interventionists to isolationists in military policy; and they went from a Keynesian spending philosophy [after economist John Maynard Keynes] to an affection for balanced budget amendments.

Whether they are pandering to the Civil Rights Movement or the Christian Right, they are both after nothing but political success.

Which of the parties will end up first pandering to the nascent [young or recent] libertarian movement remains to be seen. But it should not be the concern of the libertarians themselves, nor any of our fellow political movements looking for an institutional home. History is instructive. Once full popularity of a movement is achieved, the parties pander accordingly.

Movement More Important than Parties

While we consider conservatism to be inextricably tied to the Republican Party, it was not always that way. In the 1940s and 1950s, conservatism was a dead movement comprised of a handful of septuagenarian anti-communists. William F. Buckley changed that. His magazine, *National Review,* became the vanguard of a movement which would slowly gain the public support necessary to regain control of the Republican Party. In 1964, conservative Barry Goldwater was trounced running on a platform nearly identical to the editorial positions of *National Review.* In 1980, Ronald Reagan was elected in a landslide running on a platform nearly identical to the editorial positions of *National Review.* That's how it's done.

Decades earlier, the liberals achieved a similar impact. Before the 1930s, socialist policies were viewed as disgusting and unconstitutional in free-market America. But thanks to the writing and advocacy of *The Nation* and *The New Republic,* the socialists were able to attract a groundswell of support for regulation, extortionate taxation, nationalization, and other gems they borrowed from the Bolsheviks. This support (thanks to its American rebranding as "liberalism" instead of socialism) eventually inspired the New Deal. And thus, the lasting nuptial between the Democrats and socialism was born.

It's best to remember that parties don't adopt new movements out of ideology. They adopt them out of strategy—when they can win elections by adopting them.

EVALUATING THE AUTHORS' ARGUMENTS:

After reading this viewpoint and the one preceding it, do you believe third parties provide a service to democracy? Give reasons for your answers.

Facts About the Election Process

Primaries and Debates
According to a 2007 survey by Rasmussen Reports:
- Sixty-two percent of those surveyed say that political parties need to find a better way to nominate their presidential candidates, with 64 percent of Democrats, 54 percent of Republicans, and 68 percent of Independents saying so.
- Only 35 percent say they know the date of their state's primary election.
- Thirty-three percent say there are too many debates, 30 percent say there are not enough debates, 22 percent say the number is about right, and 15 percent are not sure.
- Fifteen percent say presidential debates are exciting, and 58 percent say they are boring. Men (63 percent) find the debates boring more often than women (54 percent). Adults under thirty are more likely to find presidential debates exciting (22 percent).
- Twenty-two percent say that debates are very important in determining how they will vote. Thirty-three percent of adults under thirty say the debates are very important to their voting decision.
- Republicans say the debates are useless by a 59 percent to 23 percent margin. Democrats say they are useless by a 43 percent to 39 percent margin. Independents say they are useless by a 50 percent to 24 percent margin.

The Integrity of the Voting Process
According to a 2007 survey by Rasmussen Reports:
- Forty-eight percent of those surveyed said elections are generally fair to voters and 37 percent said they are not fair. Seventy percent of Republicans and 31 percent of Democrats thought elections were fair.
- Seventy-seven percent of likely voters agree that displaying a photo ID should be required to cast a vote.
- Twenty-nine percent say ballots should be posted in both English and Spanish.

A 2006 survey by Rasmussen Reports found:
- Sixty-five percent of Americans say campaign finance is a very or somewhat important issue.
- Twenty-three percent of Americans favor public funding of political campaigns; 56 percent are opposed to such funding.
- Half of Americans believe it takes a contribution of at least fifty thousand dollars to influence a congressman or governor; 27 percent think it takes a contribution of at least one hundred thousand dollars to have influence.

Religion and Elections

According to a November 2007 poll by Rasmussen Reports:
- Seventy percent of those surveyed think their local religious leaders should not "suggest" which candidate to vote for, 16 percent thought religious leaders should suggest who to vote for, and 14 percent were unsure.
- Sixty-two percent of those surveyed thought it was not appropriate for a presidential candidate to campaign at religious services, 24 percent thought it was appropriate for a presidential candidate to campaign at religious services, and 14 percent were unsure.

According to a 2007 poll by research and consultation firm Greenberg Quinlan Rosner, when asked to respond to the statement "Presidential candidates should NOT use their religion or faith to influence voters to support them":
- Sixty-eight percent agreed (45 percent strongly agreeing) and 30 percent disagreed (18 percent strongly disagreeing).
- Seventy-five percent of Democrats agreed (54 percent strongly) and 24 percent disagreed (12 percent strongly); 70 percent of Independents agreed (50 percent strongly) and 28 percent disagreed (17 percent strongly); and 58 percent of Republicans agreed (28 percent strongly) and 41 percent disagreed (27 percent strongly). Nonwhite voters were slightly more likely to agree with the statement than white voters.
- Seventy-eight percent of those who did not attend religious services regularly agreed with the statement and 60 percent of those who did attend religious services regularly agreed.

Voting Patterns in the 2004 Election

According to the U.S. Census Bureau:

- Seventy-one percent of citizens in Iowa and 72 percent of citizens in New Hampshire voted in in the 2004 presidential election. Iowa is the home of the first-in-the-nation political-party caucus, and New Hampshire is the site of the first-in-the-nation party primary.
- Dixville Notch, New Hampshire, with a population of seventy-four, is traditionally one of the first communities in the nation to vote in the presidential primary season and to cast its votes on election day in November. Registered voters gather to cast their ballots at midnight, when the polls open, and polls usually close minutes later.
- Seventy-nine percent of registered voters voted in Minnesota. Other states voting at 70 percent or more include Wisconsin, Oregon, Maine, New Hampshire, North Dakota, Iowa, and Montana.
- Seventy-two percent of voting-age citizens were registered to vote in 2004, compared with 70 percent registered in 2000.
- A record 126 million people voted in the November 2004 election—the most ever for a presidential year.
- Eighty-nine percent of registered voters reported casting ballots in 2004, up from 86 percent in 2000.
- Sixty-five percent of women and 62 percent of men voted in the 2004 presidential election.
- Seventy-two percent of citizens fifty-five or older voted in the 2004 presidential election.
- Only 47 percent of persons between eighteen and twenty-four years of age voted in the 2004 presidential election, but this was an increase of 11 percentage points from 2000.
- One-fifth of voters reported voting before election day 2004—either in person or by mail.
- Twenty-four percent of voters said they registered to vote at a county or government registration office. This was the most common registration method.
- One-fifth of registered voters who did not vote in 2004 said it was because they were too busy or had conflicting work or school schedules. This was the most common reason given for not voting.
- Seventy-four percent of military veterans cast ballots in 2004, compared with 63 percent of the rest of the population.

- Eighty percent of citizens with a bachelor's degree or higher voted in 2004, compared with 56 percent of those who had only a high school diploma.
- In 2004, turnout rates for citizens were 67 percent for non-Hispanic whites, 60 percent for blacks, 44 percent for Asians and 47 percent for Hispanics (of any race). These rates were higher than the previous presidential election by five percentage points for non-Hispanic whites and three points for blacks. The voting rates for Asian and Hispanic citizens did not change significantly between elections. These data pertain to those who identified themselves as being of a single race.

Glossary

ballot: The process of voting, or the vote cast in that process.

campaign finance laws: Laws that regulate how political campaigns are directly or indirectly financed.

compulsory voting laws: Laws that make voting a legal duty.

democracy: A government in which power is invested in the people and exercised by them directly or indirectly through freely elected representatives.

disenfranchise (also **disfranchise**): To deprive a person or group of the right to vote.

election: The process of electing members of a political body.

electioneering: Taking part in an election campaign.

eligible voter: A person who meets legal requirements, such as age or residency, to register to vote.

instant runoff voting (also **ranked-choice voting**): A voting system for single-winner elections in which voters can rank candidates in order of preference. If no candidate receives a majority of first choices, the ranked choices are used to simulate a series of "runoff" elections.

negative campaigning: Electioneering that focuses on negative aspects of an opponent rather than political issues.

primary election: A preliminary election in which voters nominate candidates for an office.

registered voter: An eligible voter who has taken steps, such as filing forms with the appropriate government agency, that make it legal for that person to vote in an election.

suffrage: The right to vote.

third party: Any political party in competition with the two dominant parties in a two-party political system.

two-party system: A party system where, as in the United States, two political parties tend to dominate voting in nearly all elections.

Organizations to Contact

The editors have compiled the following list of organizations concerned with the issues debated in this book. The descriptions are derived from materials provided by the organizations. All have publications or information available for interested readers. The list was compiled on the date of publication of the present volume; the information provided here may change. Be aware that many organizations take several weeks or longer to respond to inquiries, so allow as much time as possible.

Brookings Institution
1775 Massachusetts Ave. NW
Washington, DC 20036-2188
e-mail: brookinfo@brook.edu
Web site: www.brook.edu

The Brookings Institution is a private, nonprofit organization that conducts research on economics, education, foreign and domestic government policy, and the social sciences. It publishes the quarterly *Brookings Review* and many books through its publishing division, the Brookings Institution Press. A searchable database on the Web site provides access to articles on voting and elections.

Cato Institute
1000 Massachusetts Ave. NW
Washington, DC 20001-5403
e-mail: cato@cato.org
Web site: www.cato.org

The Cato Institute is a libertarian public policy research foundation dedicated to limiting the role of government and protecting individual liberties. The Cato Institute is named after *Cato's Letters,* a series of libertarian pamphlets that Cato's founders say helped lay the philosophical foundation for the American Revolution. Cato's searchable database allows access to a number of articles on voting and elections.

The Center for Responsive Politics
1101 Fourteenth St. NW, Suite 1030
Washington, DC 20005-5635

(202) 857-0044
fax: (202) 857-7809
e-mail: info@crp.org
Web site: http://opensecrets.org

The Center for Responsive Politics tracks money in politics and its effect on elections and public policy. The center conducts computer-based research on campaign finance issues for the news media, academics, activists, and the public at large. This organization has a wealth of information about who funds political campaigns that can be accessed through the organization's searchable database.

Common Cause
1133 Nineteenth St. NW, 9th Floor
Washington, DC 20036
(202) 833-1200
Web site: www.commoncause.org

Common Cause promotes honest, open, and accountable government and citizen participation in the functioning of the U.S. government. Among the issues the group focuses on are voting, increased citizen participation, media consolidation, and campaign reform. The group's Web site has articles on these topics and information on how to register to vote.

electionline.org
1025 F St. NW, 9th Floor
Washington, DC 20004
(202) 552-2000
fax: (202) 552-2299
e-mail: info@electionline.org
Web site: www.electionline.org

Electionline.org, a project of the Pew Center on the States, is a nonpartisan, Nonadvocacy Web site providing up-to-the-minute news and analysis on election reform. The organization's searchable database has made it a leading source for journalists, policy makers, election officials, academics, and concerned citizens to learn about, discuss, and debate election administration issues.

electionreform.org
c/o Chris McGrath
1600 Wilson Blvd., Suite 800
Arlington, VA 22209

e-mail: info@electionreform.org
Web site: www.electionreform.org

The mission of this organization is to facilitate constructive and effective changes to the American election process. It maintains a Web site designed as a source of information and a forum for discussion about problems with the current election process. Of particular interest to this group are the issues of reform of the electoral college and campaign financing.

FairVote
FairVote–Center for Voting and Democracy
6930 Carroll Ave., Suite 610
Takoma Park, MD 20912
(301) 270-4616
fax: (301) 270-4133
e-mail: info@fairvote.org
Web site: www.fairvote.org

FairVote is a leading national organization acting to transform America's elections to achieve secure and universal access to participation, a full spectrum of meaningful choices, and majority rule with fair representation and a voice for all. The searchable database at FairVote's Web site provides access to news, data, and reports on voting and elections.

The Heritage Foundation
214 Massachusetts Ave. NE
Washington, DC 20002-4999
(202) 546-4400
fax: (202) 546-8328
e-mail: info@heritage.org
Web site: www.heritage.org

The Heritage Foundation is a conservative think tank that promotes public policy based on limited government and individual freedom. The organization's Web site has a searchable database that includes many articles about voting and elections, especially in countries other than the United States.

Hoover Institution
434 Galvez Mall
Stanford University
Stanford, CA 94305-6010
(650) 723-1754

fax: (650) 723-1687
e-mail: horaney@hoover.stanford.edu

The Hoover Institution promotes individual, economic, and political freedom and representative government. Its searchable Web site provides access to numerous reports and studies concerning voting and elections.

League of Women Voters (LWV)
1730 M St. NW, Suite 1000
Washington, DC 20036-4508
(202) 429-1965
fax: (202) 429-0854
e-mail: via Web site at https://member.lwv.org/ContactUs.asp
Web site: www.lwv.org

The League of Women Voters is a nonpartisan organization working at local, state, and federal levels to improve government and impact public policies through citizen education and advocacy. The league's Web site has a searchable database of information on LWV projects and voting issues as well as opportunities to take action on issues related to voting.

National Democratic Institute (NDI)
2030 M St. NW, 5th Floor
Washington, DC 20036-3306
(202) 1728-5500
fax: (202) 728-5520
e-mail: contact@ndi.org
Web site: www.ndi.org

The National Democratic Institute for International Affairs is a nonprofit organization working to strengthen democracy worldwide. Information on elections, election monitoring, and the election process can be accessed from the searchable database at the organization's Web site.

Project Vote
739 Eighth St. SE, Suite 202
Washington, DC 20003
(800) 546-8683
Web site: www.projectvote.org

Project Vote provides professional training, management, evaluation, and technical services on a broad continuum of key issues related to voter engagement and participation in low-income and minority communities. The organization's Web site has news, reports, and studies about voting and litigation concerning voting.

ReformElections.org
c/o The Century Foundation
41 E. Seventieth St.
New York, NY 10021
(212) 535-4441
fax: (212) 535-7534
e-mail: info@tcf.org
Web site: www.reformelections.org

ReformElections.org is the Century Foundation's informational Web site on election reform. In addition to the foundation's ongoing research on election reform issues, Reformelections.org features resource guides, policy developments, and the latest research from the election-reform community, accessible via the organization's searchable Web site database.

Rock the Vote
805 Twenty-first St., 401
Washington, DC 20052
e-mail: via Web site at www.rockthevote.com/rtv_contact.php
Web site: www.rockthevote.com

This organization encourages young people to register to vote and facilitates voter registration via an online voter registration form. The organization's Web site has information about voting, political issues, and elections and a blog focusing on student voting.

The Sentencing Project
514 Tenth St. NW, Suite 100
Washington, DC 20004
(202) 628-0871
fax: (202) 628-1091
Web site: www.sentencingproject.org

This nonprofit organization promotes reduced reliance on incarceration. Its Web site provides access to a lot of reports, policy analysis, and data on felony disenfranchisement, an issue of special importance to this organization.

For Further Reading

Books

Barone, Michael. *The Almanac of American Politics 2008: The Senators, the Representatives and the Governors—Their Records and Election Results, Their States and Districts.* Washington, DC: National Journal Group, 2007. An almanac describing the records and election results for elected officials.

Bendavid, Naftali. *The Thumpin': How Rahm Emanuel and the Democrats Learned to Be Ruthless and Ended the Republican Revolution.* New York: Doubleday, 2007. Describes the campaign strategy employed by Rahm Emanuel to help Democrats retake control of Congress.

Byrne, Dara N., and Editors of Black Issues in Higher Education. *The Unfinished Agenda of the Selma-Montgomery Voting Rights March.* Hoboken, NJ: John Wiley & Sons, 2005. Scholars, activists, and participants in the civil rights movement offer a testimony to the people who put their lives in jeopardy and consider what remains to be fulfilled four decades later.

Gumbel, Andrew. *Steal This Vote: Dirty Elections and the Rotten History of Democracy in America.* New York: Nation, 2005. Discusses voter fraud, vote stealing, and vote suppression in the United States during the past two hundred years.

Henneberger, Melinda. *If They Only Listened to Us: What Women Voters Want Politicians to Hear.* New York: Simon and Schuster, 2007. Describes what women voters look for in political candidates.

Norris, Pippa. *Electoral Engineering: Voting Rules and Political Behavior.* New York: Cambridge University Press, 2004. This book examines how different electoral systems affect voting behavior and shows how the rules for voting affect the outcome of elections.

Overton, Spencer. *Stealing Democracy: The New Politics of Voter Suppression.* New York: Norton, 2006. Describes how voting laws and regulations discourage, discount, and suppress voting.

Polsby, Nelson W., and Aaron Wildavsky, with David A. Hopkins. *Presidential Elections: Strategies and Structures of American Politics.*

Lanham, MD: Rowman & Littlefield, 2008. Describes strategies used to win presidential elections.

Rossi, Ann. *Created Equal: Women Campaign for the Right to Vote, 1840–1920*. Washington, DC: National Geographic, 2005. A brief history of American women's fight for the right to vote.

Rubin, Aviel David. *Brave New Ballot: The Battle to Safeguard Democracy in the Age of Electronic Voting*. New York: Morgan Road, 2006. Addressing both technical and legal problems, the author shows how easy it is to rig an election. He describes the vulnerability of computerized systems to tampering, not only by insiders like poll workers but also by outsiders able to breach the system without detection.

Sabato, Larry J., and Howard R. Ernst. *Encyclopedia of American Political Parties and Elections*. New York: Facts On File, 2006. This encyclopedia is a reference resource to issues concerning elections and political parties.

Saltman, Roy G. *The History and Politics of Voting Technology: In Quest of Integrity and Public Confidence*. New York: Palgrave Macmillan, 2006. This book discusses issues of integrity and fraud brought about by new voting technology.

Walters, Ronald. *Freedom Is Not Enough: Black Voters, Black Candidates, and American Presidential Politics*. Lanham, MD: Rowman and Littlefield, 2005. Traces the history of the black vote since 1965, celebrates its fortieth anniversary in 2005, and shows why passing a law is not the same as ensuring its enforcement, legitimacy, and opportunity.

Wattenberg, Martin P. *Is Voting for Young People?* New York: Pearson Longman, 2007. This book explores the reasons why the young are less and less likely to follow politics and vote in the United States, as well as many other established democracies, and suggests ways of changing that.

Periodicals

Anderson, John B. "Novel Idea: Let Most Popular Candidate Win; Instant Runoff Voting Is Simple and Effective," *Chicago Sun-Times*, October 1, 2007.

Averill, David. "Did Negative Campaigns Succeed? Yes," *Tulsa (OK) World*, November 12, 2006.

Barnes, Robert, and Matthew Mosk. "Justices to Consider Finance Law Limits; Campaign Issue Hits Court for 3rd Time," *Washington Post*, April 25, 2007.

Barr, Cameron W. "Security of Electronic Voting Is Condemned; Paper Systems Should Be Included, Agency Says," *Washington Post*, December 1, 2006.

Benson, Jocelyn Friedrichs. "Election Fraud and the Initiative Process: A Study of the 2006 Michigan Civil Rights Initiative," *Fordham Urban Law Journal*, April 1, 2007.

Callaghan, Peter. "Instant Runofff Poses Puzzle for Auditor," *Tacoma (WA) News Tribune*, May 29, 2007.

Century Foundation, "The Best and Worst in Election Reform, 2006," AScribe Law News Service, January 3, 2007.

Churcher, Joe. "Time to Make Voting Compulsory," *Birmingham Post (UK)*, May 1, 2006.

Cincinnati Post. "Religious Leaders Call for End of Negative Campaigning," November 9, 2007.

Economist. "Election Forensics," February 24, 2007.

Feldmann, Linda. "Sticking Point of Voting-Reform Bid: Photo IDs; a Bipartisan Panel Urged Fixes to US Elections Monday, but Critics Object to Call for IDs," *Christian Science Monitor*, September 21, 2005.

Gordon, Greg. "Efforts to Stop 'Voter Fraud' May Have Curbed Legitimate Voting," Knight Ridder Washington Bureau, May 20, 2007.

Hoffman, Ian. "Hackers, Scientists to Probe E-Voting," *Oakland (CA) Tribune*, May 10, 2007.

Karlin, Rick. "Sides Spar over Voting Machine Rule: Push to Change the Law Pits Need to Prevent Fraud Against Desire to Protect Proprietary Software Rights," *Albany (NY) Times Union*, June 16, 2007.

Keller, Amy. "Plastic—and Paper? New Electronic Voting Machines Aren't Perfect, and Some People Around Florida Haven't Given Up on Requiring a Paper Trail as Part of the Voting Process," *Florida Trend*, October 1, 2006.

Kennedy, Jr., Robert F. "Was the 2004 Election Stolen?" *Rolling Stone*, June 1, 2006.

Kuma, Sujay. "Should You Be Casting a Vote for Chuck Norris or Oprah Winfrey?" *University Wire*, December 7, 2007.

Lambrecht, Bill, and Adam Sichko. "New Voter ID Requirements Spark Legal Battles, Confusion," *St. Louis Post-Dispatch*, September 16, 2006.

Mosk, Matthew, and Sarah Cohen. "Campaigns Raise, Burn More Cash, More Quickly; Rapid Spending Puts Some in Jeopardy Early," *Washington Post*, July 16, 2007.

Northway, Wally. "Negative Political Campaigns: Ultimate Love-Hate Relationships?" *Mississippi Business Journal*, September 3, 2007.

Philadelphia Inquirer. "Campaign-Finance Law Upheld: A Solid Blow vs. Pay to Play," April 3, 2007.

Price, Edwin Rockwell. "Rankin' Votes for Peace: Jeannette Rankin's Struggle for Peace Began and Ended with Election Reform," *Peacework*, March 1, 2006.

PR Newswire. "Midwest Reform Groups Call on FCC to Hold TV Broadcasters Accountable for Inadequate Election and Government Coverage," June 12, 2007.

Syracuse (NY) Post-Standard. "A 'Flimsy Facade'; New Report on State Campaign Finance Law Could Be a Force for Change," July 30, 2006.

Tacoma (WA) News Tribune. "Working Out the Wrinkles in a New Way of Voting," May 30, 2007. www.prnewswire.com.

Tucker, Brian. "Positively Tired of Negative Campaigning," *Crain's Cleveland Business*, November 6, 2006.

US Newswire. "'US Attorney-Gate' Provides Window into Effort to Suppress Minority Voting," March 29, 2007.

US Newswire. "Voter Turnout in U.S. Elections Not Increased by Early Voting Measures," October 31, 2007.

Wayment, Jacqueline. "If You Think Your Vote Doesn't Count, Read This Now," *University Wire*, November 1, 2007.

Williams, Alex. "Students Should Get Out and Vote," *University Wire*, November 1, 2007.

Zajac, Andrew, and Tim Jones. "More States Ask Voters to Show ID: As Laws Multiply, So Do Debates About Whether They Stop Voter Fraud—or Voting," *Chicago Tribune*, October 31, 2006.

Web Sites

Blackboxvoting.com (http://blackboxvoting.com). This Web site provides news and reports concerning electronic voting fraud, as well as links to other Web sites pertaining to the same subjects.

Democratic National Committee (www.dnc.org). Site provides information and news about election issues and the opportunity to become involved from a Democratic perspective.

Electiononline.org (www.electiononline.org). The searchable database is a great resource for up-to-the-minute news and analysis on election reform.

FairVote (www.fairvote.org). The searchable database at FairVote's Web site provides access to news, data, and reports on voting and elections.

MoveOn.org (www.moveon.org). Site provides information and news about election issues and the opportunity to become involved from a progressive perspective.

Republican National Committee (www.rnc.org). Site provides information and news about election issues and the opportunity to become involved from a Republican perspective.

Index

Picture Credits

AP Images 11, 15, 21, 25, 32, 35, 43, 45, 49, 52, 60, 64, 71, 77, 79, 84, 87, 96, 103, 108, 116

Steve Zmina, 16, 20, 27, 37, 41, 48, 55, 58, 66, 82, 89, 94, 101, 110, 115